Making Friends among the Taliban

"The more people find moral meaning in telling the stories of Dan Terry's work, the better they are equipped to promote peace. I suspect Dan would not want us to remember him as a saint. But . . . we can certainly remember him as a hero of the age."
—*Michael Semple, leading practitioner of conflict resolution in Afghanistan and South Asia; from the foreword*

"Dan Terry sought the back seat in tea shops across Afghanistan to practice 'small talk as peacemaking,' insisting on the good in all people. A powerful and vivid tribute."
—*Doug Pritchard, former co-director, Christian Peacemaker Teams*

"Dan Terry proved that even the most desperate circumstances can yield hope and understanding. Jonathan Larson pays tribute to a remarkable man, recounting episodes that are as truly improbable as they are inspiring."
—*Stephen Alter, author of* Amritsar to Lahore: Crossing the India-Pakistan Border

Making Friends among the Taliban

A Peacemaker's Journey in Afghanistan

Jonathan P. Larson

Herald Press

Harrisonburg, Virginia
Waterloo, Ontario

Library of Congress Cataloging-in-Publication Data
Larson, Jonathan P., 1947–
    Making friends among the Taliban: a peacemaker's journey
in Afghanistan / by Jonathan P. Larson.
        p. cm.
    ISBN 978-0-8361-9665-8 (pbk:. alk. paper) 1. Terry, Dan,
1946-2010. 2. Humanitarian assistance—Afghanistan. 3. Taliban.
4. Afghanistan—Social life and customs. 5. Americans—
Afghanistan—Biography. 6. Social workers—Afghanistan—
Biography. I. Title.
    HV40.32.T386L37 2012
    958.104'71—dc23
    [B]
                                                    2012028172

Unless otherwise noted, Scripture text is quoted, with per-
mission, from the New Revised Standard Version, © 1989,
Division of Christian Education of the National Council of
Churches of Christ in the United States of America.

MAKING FRIENDS AMONG THE TALIBAN
Copyright © 2012 by Herald Press, Harrisonburg, Virginia 22802
    Released simultaneously in Canada by Herald Press,
    Waterloo, Ontario N2L 6H7. All rights reserved.
Library of Congress Control Number: 2012028172
International Standard Book Number: 978-0-8361-9665-8
Printed in United States of America
Cover design by Reuben Graham, design by Josh Byler
Cover photos provided by Mennonite Mission Network

To order or request information, please call 1-800-245-7894 in
the U.S. or 1-800-631-6535 in Canada.
Or visit www.heraldpress.com.

16 15 14 13 12   10 9 8 7 6 5 4 3 2 1

This volume of stories belongs to the courageous Afghans who told them out of wonder and affection for their friend, Dantri.

Contents

Dan Terry, "Dantri" to his Afghan friends. Photograph used by permission of CURE International.

Foreword

by Michael Semple

There is a ramshackle Sufi shrine on the outskirts of Islamabad, Pakistan. It is a jumble of trees, huts, dovecotes, graves, prayer terraces, water tanks, and spiritual bric-a-brac. It has always been an informal gathering place, attracting alike itinerant *Malang* holy men, tired shoppers, and regular worshipers. A barbed wire fence has recently appeared, ringing the complex and channelling visitors to prescribed entrances.

The barbed wire is a sign of our troubled times, when people conclude that the informality of the open door invites trouble. The shrine strikes me as a metaphor for Dan Terry—its sprawling vibrancy evoking Dan's chaotically joyful approach to life. But the abrupt appearance of the barbed wire begs the question of whether the time for us to live as Dan did has passed. The connection is not just metaphorical; Islamabad's incongruous fence builders are trying to secure local worshipers from the same armed bigotry that killed Dan and his companions. But Dan lived his life and found meaning beyond the wire.

I struggle to encapsulate concisely the spirit of Dan Terry. Adjectives tumble out . . . joyful, loving, spiritual, helpful, practical, searching, confused, humorous, accident-prone, gentle, interested, adventurous, chaotic, fun, and fundamentally good. I can testify to Jonathan Larson's triumph in collating the tales of Dan Terry's life, because every one of those adjectives is illustrated in his narrative. Close your eyes and Dan bounds from the pages.

As one who has scaled mountains and cajoled jeeps out of muddy ruts with Dan, I also search for the deeper meaning of the narratives. Dan's companions in Afghanistan and the world outside have told their stories, and Jonathan has masterfully woven them into a coherent life. As a companion I can testify that the tales capture the true spirit of the man. But they also exude a hint of heroic lore.

To puzzle out how an imaginatively recounted narrative can construct a true life, I refer the reader to one of the masterpieces of modern anthropology of Afghanistan: David Edwards's *Heroes of the Age*. In Peshawar, Pakistan, in the 1980s, David found sixteen Afghans to tell him part of the life story of Hudda Mullah, a Muslim saint who lived in Dan's stomping ground of eastern Afghanistan in the second half of the nineteenth century. Most informants were descendants of the Mullah's original companions, and their stories were a heady blend of the magical and the historical. Edwards solved the puzzle by concluding that "all stories moralize the history with which they are concerned . . . implying a process of perception and interpretation by which meaning was attached to events."

Dan Terry lived his life generously and joyfully in Afghanistan during a period when famine, coups, revolution, war, and displacement shook society to its foundations. Amid these upheavals Afghans struggled to find their moral compass. Dan's joyful morality was deeply reassuring to people whose very worldview was threatened by the evil they saw around them. Dan was a good man in bad times. In sharing his spirituality and practical skills, he brightened the lives of many people blighted by difficult times.

The parallels between narratives of Dan Terry and the Muslim saint Hudda Mullah bring us to another essential facet of Dan's life. Dan lived out his Christian spirituality surrounded and accepted by Afghan Muslims. Jonathan rightly quotes Afghans praising Dan for embodying all the characteristics they would expect of a good Muslim. It is worth dwelling on how Dan won this particular accolade. Dan was a devoted Christian whose path to God involved serving humanity and living morally. He knew that Christianity and Islam share 99 percent of their moral DNA. Away from the front line, Dan delighted in helping good Afghans cope with challenges familiar to his compatriots—like a famous village discussion in Lal wa Sar Jangal over long hair and rebellious teenagers. Dan's good-natured championing of humanity and morality against their dark opposites so closely united Muslim and Christian that the labels lost their power to divide.

Another point that might trouble those who did not know Dan is his relaxed relationship with the Taliban. We have long been told that the Taliban incarnate evil. Dan's discovery that many Afghan Taliban retain their sense of morality and even a spirit of service was important in charting the common ground which may yet prove the basis of a peace among Afghans—a peace that Dan believed was possible. Afghans and the world at large have a stake in finding that common ground and ending the debilitating conflict.

But how do we make sense of the last tale of Dan Terry's life? Did evil triumph when fanatics machine-gunned Dan and his companions against the backdrop of beautiful mountain scenery? I think not. As I was contemplating Dan's life for this foreword, I was interrupted by a call from a senior Muslim jurist and Taliban religious scholar. His rambling conversation mixed humor, an optimistic tale of something accidentally going right, and an exposition of how the ideal Afghan Muslim society would protect all religious groups with space for all to serve. The peacemaking spirit of Dan Terry lives on in such words. And the more people find moral meaning in telling the stories of Dan's work, the better they are equipped to promote peace. I suspect Dan would not want us to remember him as a saint. But in the sense conveyed by Edwards, we can certainly remember him as a hero of the age.

—Michael Semple is a scholar and practitioner focused on conflict resolution in Afghanistan and South Asia. He is a senior fellow at the Carr Center for Human Rights Policy at Harvard Kennedy School and has previously worked for the European Union and United Nations.

Acknowledgments

An old jazz saxophonist was once asked, "Where, pray tell, does the music that flows from your sax come from?" He answered tersely, "I'm just trying to say thank you." As the scribe of the stories that follow, I can only pray that gratitude on my part has produced a worthy telling, that something of their native melodies has survived.

It grieves me that I am constrained from naming the brilliant Afghans, who, at some risk to themselves, told many of the spirited tales about Dan Terry that follow. These stories might well make targets of their tellers were their identities known, so I have removed any detail that might bring grief to them or their families. I believe a day will come when they will be free to tell these stories—which they can do more artfully than I—and it will no longer be necessary to leave individuals nameless in the telling.

This story could not have been told without the understanding of the Terry family: Seija, Dan's wife, who deftly connected me with people in Kabul; their daughters, Hilja, Anneli, and Saara; and their respective families. Despite their sense of loss and busy lives of their own, they humored my curiosity and delving and offered unguarded access to family archives and photographs. Their experiences as a family beg a fuller telling.

I am indebted to Kate Clark, of measured insight and generous spirit, who opened doors for me in Kabul and brought me into partnership with Rohullah Sorush, my able Afghan interpreter, companion, and guide. I have also valued the reflections of Michael Semple, an Irish scholar and journalist devoted to charting a peaceable future not only for Afghanistan but for the entire region.

In the quiet background of this account are a host of humanitarians, Dan's peers, who go on serving in anonymity (and harbor some misgivings about the unwanted attention this telling of Dan's story might attract). I found the staff of CURE's international hospital network and Kabul guesthouse especially congenial. Among them, Dale Brantner, Rick Manning, Keith Rose, Jerry Umanos, and Philip and Jennifer Adams deserve grateful mention.

Gary Moorehead of the Marigold Foundation, who found inspiration in Dan's example and has invested himself in remote Afghanistan, readily shared his memories of Dan.

Jim Couch and Warrick Gilbert of the International Assistance Mission (IAM), with which Dan worked for many years, warmly welcomed and encouraged me and freely offered their recollections.

Dan's lifelong comrades—Dan'l Taylor of Future Generations, Jennifer Ide, and their son Luke—were dangerously affirming and put me in their debt, as did a warm circle of friends from Woodstock School in India, which Dan and I attended together. Also supportive was the fraternity of church workers in South Asia who knew the Terry family. Deserving special notice is Peggy Alter, who recognized the beauty and worth of this story early on and took every opportunity to strengthen its telling.

It was surely providential that I came to the attention of those at MennoMedia and The Center for Justice and Peacebuilding at Eastern Mennonite University who watch for stories of lived faith in search of peace and laid claim to this narrative. Amy Gingerich, Byron Rempel-Burkholder, Reuben Graham, Karen Campbell, and especially my editor, Valerie Weaver-Zercher, helped to bring the story coherently to term.

Lastly, I am beholden to members of my family, who have been unfailing in their interest and stalwart in their belief that this telling is worth the exertions. Chief among those has been my wife, Mary Kay, who stubbornly thinks better of me than either my work or I deserve.

100 mi
200 km

TURKMENISTAN

DUSHANBE

TAJIKISTAN

• Mashed

Balkh   Kunduz   Faizabad

Shebergan   Mazar-i-Sharif   3   • Sarhad

Dara-i-Suf
          • Bekh   Sharron Valley

Yakaolang   2   Parún

• Herat   • Bamian   KABUL   Serobi   1
Lal wa   • Jalalabad   Khyber Pass
Sar Jangal   • Peshawar

          Ghanzi   • Gardez   ISLAMABAD

          • Kandahar

IRAN   PAKISTAN

          •Quetta

1. Laghman province
2. Nuristan province
3. Badakhshan province

Region occupied by
the Hazara ethnic group

Region of the
Hindu Kush

AFGHANISTAN

Introduction

Rescued Marbles

The haunting news of the death of Dan Terry and nine colleagues in the backcountry of Afghanistan reached me in a coffee shop in small-town Indiana in August 2010. It was the same town where my wife, Mary Kay, and I had been married forty-one years earlier, when Dan had turned up breathless at the last moment to be our best man. That summer in 1969, the very weekend of the Woodstock rock festival, Dan had passed up an epic frolic to the rhythms of Janis Joplin, choosing instead to play his part at our sedate Mennonite wedding. He arrived with wedding gifts conveying his affection: matching rucksacks.

Mary Kay and I shouldered those packs and set out for the lake country of central Africa, the Ruwenzori Mountains, and later the Kalahari Desert. As for Dan, he laced up his Henke boots and disappeared into the Hindu Kush, the mountain range curled between central Afghanistan and northern Pakistan. He was a terrible correspondent, but every once in a great while he would surface with his wife, Seija, and their family, and our paths would cross for a handful of hours. We would pass the night swapping improbable tales of India, Africa, and Afghanistan: of places beyond beautiful but also full of struggle and suffering. After our brief reunions, we would go our divergent paths, but I always had a lingering sense that Dan's most pungent and remarkable stories had been left untold somewhere in mountain country.

Dan's love affair with the Hindu Kush was kindled in the foothills of the Indian Himalayas, where, as the son of Methodist missionaries, he tramped ridges and valleys, swam the icy tributaries of the Ganges, and sipped *chai* in mountain tea shops with charcoal porters, with farmers, and with us, his frequent trailmates. Also the child of post-war missionaries, I attended school in India with Dan and later wandered with him through the bazaars of fabled Afghan cities such as Kandahar, Herat, and Jalalabad. I sensed faintly how his imagination was already being taken captive by this land, a place marked with a pathos he would one day come to share.

Dan moved on to Central Asia as a young adult and in time acquired the Afghan name *Dantri*. In Afghanistan, he pursued his humanitarian work with scant concern for his personal safety amid famine, prison, and, occasionally, rifle muzzles. A furnace-like passion and unswerving drive for bridge building set him apart from the bloody themes of both empire past and the present war. "In Afghanistan, I feel less intimidated or dispossessed the less I intimidate or hold others in contempt," Dan once wrote to school friends. "Categorical 'enemies' have rescued me, and more than my marbles, again and again."

In the aftermath of the 2010 killings that ended Dan's life, it occurred to me that those rescued marbles might be well worth weighing up, particularly the stories of Dan's decades of wandering the mountains in Afghan company. In that Indiana coffee shop where the news of Dan's death broke with such finality, curiosity about those phantom stories took root in my imagination. Those who knew Dan at all had worried that

his story might well come to such an ending—a pos-
sibility that he had accepted as worth the joy of his
peacemaker calling.

Growing curiosity took me to Afghanistan in
October 2011, a little over a year after Dan, seven
other foreign aid workers, and two Afghans met their
end while returning to Kabul from a medical trip. The
deaths of Dan Terry, Mahram Ali, Cheryl Beckett,
Daniela Beyer, Brian Carderelli, Thomas L. Grams,
Ahmed Jawed, Glen D. Lapp, Tom Little, and Karen
Woo commanded world headlines, yet the motives
and identities of the gunmen remain to this day poorly
understood. But more than the account of the killings,
the drama of Dan's three decades of life and work in
Afghanistan intrigued me.

I found Kabul a city dusted with war. War wagons
on patrol rumbled down the chute-like streets, and
razor wire crowned the perimeter walls of warlord
mansions. Despite a rash of assassinations and bombings, Dan's Afghan friends and coworkers filtered out
of the bazaars and neighborhoods one by one to tell
me their tales of friendship and adventure with Dantri.
Eyes flashing, voices rising and then falling to a whis-
per, with gestures like sacred calligraphy, they told
stories with an unselfconscious artistry. These accounts
from Dantri's friends form the spine of the collection
that follows.

The gathering of oral narrative is an exacting
exercise in any setting. But in the context of war and
across frontiers of language and culture, hazards litter
the field. Wherever possible these stories have been cor-
roborated by multiple witnesses, who often confirmed
the findings of scholars that oral societies transmit such
accounts with astonishing fidelity.

There is something lofty and irresistible in the
stories I heard, something reminiscent of the majestic
crags in photographs of the Sharron Valley, the scene
of the killings. The dynamic driving these tales runs

something like this: to whom much is given, much is required. Dan knew that he had been lavishly endowed with faith, friendship, family, opportunity, learning, and hope. His chosen course says he'd be damned if that legacy failed to count for something.

Borne along by such a hunger and vision, Dan seemed intent not so much on healing—or even redemption—but rather on reconciliation. So it was that he counted among his friends the Taliban commanders of his neighborhood, insisting they were not the caricatures of evil portrayed in the West. Flint-like in his belief that there was something noble in each neighbor, Dan kept reaching for the humanity of each person he met. It was this credo that made him a joyful friend of the forgotten poor of the Hindu Kush and beyond. Of that rich and grand pattern of life he was often heard to say, "In the end, we're all knotted into the same carpet."

Dan himself would have bridled at interest in the small swatch of carpet that represents his life. Had he known that I would someday write a book tracing the weave of those years, he would certainly have administered a slap upside the head and let out his trademark chortle, "*Arre basht!*" Then, a grin getting the best of him, he would have shouldered his rucksack and strode away, his eye trained on some piece of rugged country ahead.

1

Chosen by Afghanistan

I

Brass samovars of sweet, milky tea mark the quarter of Peshawar, Pakistan, that has long been called *Qissa Khwani*, or the "storytellers' bazaar." Though the tea shops are cloaked in fumes from the diesel trucks that have replaced the camel caravans, *Qissa Khwani* still stands for powerful stories that have fashioned the culture, identity, and worldview of this place. The tea and stories of these shops—whether in Qissa Khwani, Kandahar, Herat, Kabul, or countless smaller mountain towns—induce a camaraderie that seems a rare, stolen comfort against the backdrop of the region's clamor.

Daniel Terry, of unkempt hair and beard and rangy frame draped in the traditional *salwar kameez*,[1] often frequented these tea shops across Central Asia. He knew they served up a good deal more than sweet mountain brew. There the stories were spun. There the proverbs were rehearsed, often with bitter laughter. There ancient

---

1. *Salwar kameez*: traditional trousers and tunic worn by Afghan men

wisdom, fates, and prophecies were remembered. The tea shop served as apt school for the curious foreign infidel. But Dan—who in time acquired an Afghan version of his name, *Dantri*—was rarely content to remain in the cheery and reputable streetside seating of the tea shops. His instinct was to drift toward the back of the shop, where the sketchiest travelers would be murmuring over the gurgle of a *hookah*.[2] Dan would offer some self-deprecating remark in Dari or Pashtu and settle himself next to those master storytellers of the tea shop shadows. When he would finally rise to excuse himself, he would be braced not only by the tea and stories but also by something rarer still: improbable friendship.

Dan and his tea shop companions would meet again somewhere—perhaps in earnest give-and-take over a hostage release, the safe passage of a truck laden with grain, or a roadside standoff. Perhaps they would come face-to-face in a blizzard, or when he was seeking agreement from village elders for a new clinic. Then they would know each other as mountain tea shop neighbors. And, as Dan would say, "You can build something with that." Even fashion a peace.

II

Follow the fabled road leading west-northwest from the tea shops of Qissa Khwani to the outskirts of Peshawar. The road traces a hairpin history paved with glory, breakneck ambition, and a generous measure of folly. A sign along the way once read, "Anybody who was ever anybody passed this way."

Past the old Kabuli Gate, the road leads you through fields and orchards and then climbs into rugged country. It runs past ruined ramparts, even a Buddhist *stupa*,[3] and then up to a rocky mountain passage: the Khyber

---

2. *Hookah*: a water pipe used for smoking tobacco

3. *Stupa*: a place of worship, typically in a mound-like shape, that contains Buddhist relics

Pass. Beyond lie the storied ranges of the Hindu Kush, the ancient Silk Route, and the vast mountain knot of Central Asia. Like the colonial British redcoats, conquerors Darius, Alexander, Genghis Khan, Tamerlane, and Babur left their footprints and sometimes their tattered honor along this stony route.

Against this vast panorama, Dan's journeys left but little trace—except upon him. There was hardly anything about the majestic peaks and ridges, the grudging valleys, or the defiance and lore of the people who call Afghanistan home that failed to set his imagination aflame. A friend of Dan's puts it this way: "Dan did not choose Afghanistan. No, Afghanistan chose him."

Dan's fierce bond with Afghanistan had been prepared, laid up like kindling. As a boy he traveled with his Methodist parents, Patricia and George, from

Pennsylvania to north India, where they lived for long stretches under the Himalayan eaves. His father crisscrossed the subcontinent as an auditor of mission schools and hospitals, sometimes spanning the great distances at the helm of a single-engine aircraft.

Dan spent his childhood and adolescence in the northern hill town of Mussoorie, India. Nothing pleased him quite so much as striding the foothills, sweaty and red-faced, following the trails of Nepali milkmen and donkey caravans that toiled along to the tinkle of their bells. To the north and east he could see the roof of that Himalayan world, whose summits were first crested in those very years by the likes of Tenzing Norgay and Edmund Hillary.

As a youngster in newly independent India, Dan also heard the stories of that pilgrim of moral heights, Mohandas Gandhi. Though felled by an assassin's bullet in 1948, Gandhi lived on in the memory of a nation that could still hear his summons to *satyagraha*, the peaceable struggle for justice. Dan also crossed the path of the young Dalai Lama, who visited Dan's classroom after a harrowing mountain escape from Lhasa, awakening Dan and his schoolmates to the struggle of the Tibetan people.

Those stories, shot through with heroic calling, resonated with what Dan observed in his own parents. His father, a conscientious objector during World War II, had served in an American mental hospital rather than join the military. It was the momentum of their convictions that eventually carried George and Patricia into missionary service in post-war India, and the footings of those convictions were writ large in the lecture halls and classrooms of Woodstock School, where Dan was a student. Beyond Pythagoras, Newton, Melville, and the Ramayana, Dan heard the thunder of biblical prophets: "Let justice roll down like waters, and righteousness like an everflowing stream" (Amos 5:24), and "The wolf shall live with the lamb . . . the calf

The young Dalai Lama (back row, second from right) visits Woodstock School in 1959 or 1960. Dan Terry is in the middle of the front row; Jonathan Larson (author) is on the far left in the last seated row. Other adults standing in the back include the school principal, members of the Tibetan entourage, and local Indian officials. Photograph by Thukral and Sons.

and the lion and the fatling together, and a little child shall lead them" (Isaiah 11:6). From the Gospels, Dan memorized the phrases from Matthew 5 that Gandhi found so stirring: "Blessed are the poor in spirit . . . Blessed are the peacemakers."

III

Dan's childhood imagination teemed with machines. He never tired of sketching rakish planes or plowing his toy Land Rovers and snub-nosed World War II trucks through the dirt crevices and rocky terrain around the family's mountain cottage, dreaming of smoky power and speed.

Such play, though, slowly gave way to an early adolescent suspicion of girls, whom he found unsettling. Unlike the toy railroad he had lovingly built, the world of cross-gender relationships seemed risky, even dangerous.

Demonstrating his capacity to lead—if not always in directions that reassured his Woodstock teachers—Dan framed a way to deal with these emerging problems of adolescence. At one point he devised an elaborate scheme to quarantine himself and his school friends from girls. They decided that even incidental contact with girls was defiling and that conversation between boys in solidarity with this scheme and any girls was taboo. Dismayed teachers at Woodstock struggled with classroom management, since Dan's plan meant that any mixed-gender activities—even, for example, forays for collection of monsoon fern specimens—foundered. The boys' silent solidarity left school administrators nonplussed and frustrated.

One day the girls countered with a culinary peace plan. They made a batch of brownies, which they presented to the boys as a peace offering. The boys—and their leader, Dan—recognized this for the Trojan horse that it was. Although most were school boarders and had not tasted homemade goodies for months, they left their brownies untouched on their desks at day's end. Even the principal, a stern Anglican clergyman of persuasive powers, failed to crack this wall of adolescent resistance. Dan's remarkable hold among his peers did not give way until hormones mercifully accomplished what eloquent appeals and threats could not.

As an adult, Dan later observed that heaven's retribution for this scheme was to grant him three daughters, with whom he made lavish and exuberant amends.

IV

"He was a master of chaos theory," one coworker says about Dan. The capacities to thrive in highly unpredictable environments, and to make friends with the prospect of surprise, Dan came by quite honestly. Indeed,

The twin peaks of Bandar Poonch in the Himalayas are visible from the ridge in Mussoorie, India, where Dan grew up. The Yamuna River rises in the Bandar Poonch glaciers.

he was thoroughly apprenticed in them by his harum-scarum family.

One day Dan, his father, George, and some friends decided to raft the upper reaches of the sacred Yamuna River, northwest of Mussoorie. The road winds down steeply, past terraced fields to a river running between narrow valley walls. The group carried a borrowed inflatable dingy to the water's edge, launched it, and soon was swept away in laughter and white water.

The beauty of the canyon walls, the river's energy, and the battle to control the bobbing, spinning raft kept others from noticing what George began to see; the raft had a leak and was slowly collapsing in the roiling current. Left unchecked, the craft would eventually collapse on the rafters. Yet many miles remained.

In desperation, the group guided the raft to the valley wall, where they scrambled out onto difficult terrain. But they could not abandon the raft, for although crippled, it would have to be returned to its owner. While the rest of the party climbed away to the road to improvise a way out, George insisted on riding the raft solo out of the mountains. He shouted to them that he would meet them where the river emerged from the canyon. With that, Dan's father was swept away beyond earshot.

After hitching a ride, Dan and the rest of the party gathered downstream at the river's edge where the mountains give way to the Doon Valley. They scoured the Yamuna's banks for any sign of George or the raft. Some began to wonder how they would organize a search or, in the worst case, convey dreadful news to the family.

Finally, as daylight faded, they heard a shout from the riverbank and saw the raft come sluicing out of the mountains, completely at the mercy of the current. Inside, nearly hidden from view, George was lying spread-eagle on the floor, holding the sagging raft open with his arms and legs fully extended.

This was not the only time the family barely survived to tell tales. After one of their periodic visits to North America, Dan's parents and sister, Ruth set out for India, while Dan remained ensconced in university studies in Kansas. George, Pat, and Ruth picked up a single-engine aircraft in Europe, intending to fly it back to South Asia for use in George's work. Loaded with gear and personal effects, they set out eastward, making hops around the Mediterranean and across western Asia, bound for India.

While crossing southern Afghanistan, they were startled when the plane's radio crackled to life as Afghan officials ordered them to break off their route and divert immediately to Kabul. Air Force jets were scrambled to escort them to the capital. Once on the ground, Dan's parents and sister were informed they had violated a strictly controlled military air corridor, although this had not appeared on any of George's navigational charts. George apologized, pleading that his error was entirely innocent and that he was only returning with his family to their place of assignment in India.

It was some days before the authorities were satisfied that Dan's father was telling the truth. They reluctantly agreed that the Terrys could proceed—but they would not be allowed to return south. Instead, they were obliged to fly directly eastward from Kabul to avoid repeating their earlier blunder.

George explained to the authorities that his plane would not be able to safely overfly the mountains separating him from Pakistan and India. Given the limitations of his aircraft and the weight of his freight and passengers, attempting such a route would be an invitation to calamity. But the authorities were in no mood to be cajoled.

With no options left, George fueled the plane lightly to avoid unnecessary weight. He said a prayer as he, Patricia, and Ruth lifted off and banked east under the watchful eye of Kabul air traffic control. For a time they paralleled the ridges, hoping they would find thermals that would lift them over the mountain crags. As George searched for updrafts, Patricia and Ruth began pitching items out of the plane in a last-ditch measure to lighten their load and gain altitude. At last, George caught a thermal that, with the lightened load, just lifted the plane over the watershed and sent them safely on their way to the Punjab.

Dan's parents later returned to the scene of this desperate hour when George agreed to lead the International Assistance Mission (IAM) in Kabul, the agency under which his son would also come to serve.

Improvising a way in the face of long and chaotic odds came naturally to the son of such a family.

V

As Dan's graduation in India from Woodstock School approached in the summer of 1965, his family made plans to return to North America. Considering conventional travel by ship or plane altogether too tame—a lost opportunity to test their mettle—the Terry family decided to cross Asia and Europe by road. After Dan's

graduation they would set out from India, drive over-
land to Rotterdam, and then cross the Atlantic by ship
to New York. From there they would continue on to
Baker University in Kansas, where Dan was enrolled
for the fall semester.

In the post–World War II years, the road network
between Pakistan and Turkey was chancy at best.
Sometimes, signage consisted only of whitewashed oil
drums marking shifting wilderness routes. Fuel could
be adulterated and sparse, bridges were precarious,
road conditions varied with the seasons, and travelers
had to improvise accommodations. Some mountain
passages harbored barbarous sheepdogs, and in lawless
country, bandits held sway. At border crossings, edgy
officials often wheedled for *baksheesh*.[4] And should
mechanical trouble occur, procuring spare parts could
make minced meat of schedule, budget, and patience.
Coups and the eruption of border quarrels might finish
off the itinerary.

As it happened, several others expressed interest in
joining this audacious family trek, and four additional
passengers signed on for a total of eight long-distance
travelers. By then, however, George had already ordered
a five-passenger Volkswagen from Germany, for delivery to the port of Karachi. How could the additional
travelers be accommodated so late in the game?

As the party began to gather for what was starting
to resemble a major Himalayan campaign, George disappeared into the tinsmith's bazaar. He could be heard
clattering with his helpers in a nearby workshop, blow-
torch in hand. Before long he emerged, blackened with
grime but flashing a grin full of satisfaction. Into the
sunshine he pulled a custom-built trailer for luggage
and an odd rooftop carrier, fashioned of aluminum
sheeting and tubing, that would comfortably seat or

---

4. *Baksheesh*: a gratuity

sleep three riders. When fully assembled, the contraption resembled a creation from some post-apocalypse movie.

As this one-of-a-kind caravan set out on its five-thousand-mile journey to Rotterdam, it never failed to win gape-mouthed notice from shepherds, school-children, soldiers, and bazaar crowds. In several European cities it left a wake of astonished drivers and traffic gridlock. But it was the travels across Afghanistan—through Jalalabad and Kabul and past the ancient walls of Ghazni, Kandahar, and Herat—that made of Dan a helpless, florid dreamer. On this cross-continental trek and others that followed, the beauty and perils of the Hindu Kush imprinted themselves upon Dan's youthful imagination. He mused that one day he would return to these lands to lead a disaster relief unit ready to respond to earthquake, flood, epidemic, war, or famine. Little did he know how this premonition would come to pass, with its triumphs and its bitter lessons.

From his rooftop perch on the Volkswagen, Dan marveled at Afghanistan's almond and fruit orchards, grain fields, and gardens. To sustain these life-giving splendors, the Afghans had engineered a system of tunnels, or *kereze*, that conveyed water from mountain slopes to the arid valleys and villages. Piercing tunnels through stony ground took a fearsome toll on the workers, who toiled with picks and crowbars to create them: rock falls, choking dust, and over-exertion sent many diggers to early graves. In compensation for such service, the community allotted the builders the best it had of honor and goods.

Dan, who clearly admired such heroic self-giving, had little inkling at the time of how much he would come to resemble the *kereze* diggers: those who work in harsh, underground settings for the life and peace of Afghan kin.

VI

Having finished his undergraduate studies in Kansas and sensing that the wild calling he had always dreamed of was now within reach, he set out in 1971 for a volunteer assignment at a new clinic serving the Hazara people of central Afghanistan. He earned his stripes at Lal wa Sar Jangal, a settlement in Ghor Province at the geographical center of Afghanistan. He used his hands and gifts in organizing the construction of buildings, opening an airstrip, capping springs, and (his first love) maintaining and providing motor transport in the mountains. With ingenuity and improvisation, in those early years he learned to fashion solutions to challenges beyond the reach of expert help, conventional wisdom, and the supply chain.

The need to muddle through daunting challenges provided a venue for Dan's deeper romance: learning Dari (Afghanistan's version of the Persian language) and coming to know the daily life of his Afghan neighbors. He never failed to invite neighbors to his table

On a trek across Europe and Asia in 1970, Dan poses in jest with a VW van at a washed-out bridge somewhere in Afghanistan. Photograph by Dan'l Taylor, used with permission.

and to friendship. In turn, he learned to be an appreciative and deferential guest among the Hazaras, both great and poor. Dan's capacity to befriend and serve prepared him for the role of the *rahnama*—a trusted guide and go-between who gently nudges travelers on their way through uncharted terrain toward a more peaceable country.

To be effective in the role of *rahnama*, Dan learned the art of hanging out with people and setting aside personal destinations for the sake of the itineraries of others. Being a *rahnama* requires curiosity about a community's fears and anxieties and attentiveness to the wisdom expressed in its stories and humor. It sometimes even requires lying awake in the darkness of Himalayan nights, pondering a people's conundrums and dilemmas.

In these early years, Dan also came to appreciate and practice what he called "positive opportunism." As he remarked, "Intentionality and system are beautiful things . . . but on the other hand, we also want to be spontaneous, exuberant, and opportunistic in a positive way." He sometimes illustrated this with a homely—and no doubt firsthand—example. "You can have a successful public health education event by just getting a flat tire somewhere, and a crowd of people will gather." A roadside mishap transformed into a golden opportunity for the betterment of a community represents perfectly Dan's emerging vision of method and work.

For Dan, community development included himself. Aware of his own foibles and the danger of untested assumptions, he was ruthless in self-examination, challenging his own motivations and remaining attentive to stirrings of his conscience. "Find a worthy concept and ram it down your own throat," he would say. He learned how devilishly slippery development work can be, how quickly everything can veer off course, and how the best intentions can proceed to a dead end. No field of work is more liable to the law of unintended consequences. He once described its precariousness this way: "It's like trying to change the flat tire on a Land Rover—while it's still rolling." The manuals have no directions for such eventualities.

Dan's remote mountain outpost in Hazara country was also the ground for his acquaintance with Seija Meilonen, a resourceful Finnish Lutheran nurse who had come to serve in the new clinic he helped to build and whom in time he would marry. Their budding affection and partnership were framed by a shared calling, a willingness to ignore hardship in light of the thrill of discovery and friendship, aspiration for a lived faith, and the chance to do work that mattered immensely.

But, as often happened in the following decades, the course of Dan's personal life was subject to the convulsions of a nation. When the king of Afghanistan, Zahir Shah, lost his dynastic throne in 1973, a fragile thread holding the country together snapped and the country plunged into turmoil. Political events scattered the team of workers at Lal wa Sar Jangal—Dan to Bangladesh and then to North America, and Seija to her home in Finland.

VII

Sent packing from the promise of such beginnings, Dan found consolation and a home with longtime friends in the Appalachian Mountains near Franklin, West Virginia. Seija, for her part, turned her time in Finland to profit by training as a midwife, acquiring skills she knew Afghan families needed.

So it was that by force of circumstance Dan and Seija romanced each other by telephone—the slopes of Spruce Knob, West Virginia, whispering to Helsinki. But they were not alone. Party lines were still the norm for many West Virginia mountain communities, and occasional sounds on the line betrayed the fact that others were listening in on their intercontinental conversations. Since little could be done about the eavesdroppers, Dan and Seija would strategically switch into Dari, the language that Persian poets adore for its powers of artful expression.

One day, while running errands in the town of Franklin, Dan learned firsthand the hazards of straddling the hemispheres. In town he encountered an elderly woman, a mountain neighbor, who solemnly informed him that in Pendleton County, speaking foreign languages on the telephone was considered rude.

2

Kebabs with a Captor

I

After a prolonged period of political churning, Soviet forces arrived in Afghanistan in 1979, and humanitarian workers were once again welcomed in the country. Dan and Seija, now married and the parents of a daughter, were able to return to Afghanistan. Since it was not possible for them to resume their work in the provinces, where armed resistance to Russian occupation was taking hold, the Terrys settled in Kabul. But trouble was never far away, even in the confines of the capital city.

In Kabul, Dan and Seija lived next door to a Finnish nurse, a longtime friend of Seija's, and her Dutch husband. This couple's two small children were playmates of Hilja, the Terrys' daughter. On a winter morning in early 1981, a frantic worker appeared at Dan and Seija's door to say he feared something terrible had happened at the neighbors' house. He and Dan found the doors to the house locked, but they eventually forced an entry. They found the couple dead on their kitchen floor, with signs of a ghastly struggle everywhere. In a closet, consumed with terror, cowered the couple's young daughter and son. The Terrys took the children into their care until extended family arrived to take them back to Europe.

The aftermath of these killings underscored the country's descent, again, into disarray. Workers with the International Assistance Mission (IAM), as happened now and again, were evacuated from Afghanistan for safety and to reconsider if their work and purposes were still viable. Meanwhile, with little grasp of Afghan realities, the newly arrived Soviet KGB opened an investigation into the murders. Numerous innocent Afghans were rounded up, mistreated, and later released for lack of evidence. The theory emerged of a robbery gone horribly wrong, but the guilty parties escaped the fraying force of the law.

A spreading sense of helplessness and disorder discredited the succession of hapless political leaders and governments who promised one by one to restore sanity. Their unkept promises would give rise to a regime that would successfully restore civil order and enforce a justice of its own: the Taliban.

II

During Soviet occupation in the late 1980s, periods of relative tranquility reigned in some quarters of Afghanistan, even while the *mujahedeen*[1] pursued guerilla warfare in others. After the failure of the Soviet project, the proud Red Army, having been humbled in the mountains, rumbled back home across the bridges in defeat in early 1989.

With the collapse of Russia's client regime, ethnic warlords seized what they could of their home turf, taking up cudgels against each other in the heaving of personal and

---

1. *Mujahedeen*: Islamic resistance fighters backed by the United States and other governments

tribal politics. Kabul
fell under protracted
siege, and rockets
rained from the sur-
rounding ridges onto
terrified residents. The
capital was carved
into warring districts,
paralyzing commerce
and city services. Life
took on a desperate,
medieval air as resi-
dents struggled for the
means of survival.

The Terry fam-
ily—a fivesome when
their daughters, Hilja,
Anneli, and Saara,
returned periodically
from boarding school
in India—learned to

The Terry family in 1996. Left to right: Seija,
Saara, Dan, Hilja, Anneli.

cope with life balanced on a shuddering knife edge and even
managed a touch of humor. When bombardment began,
they would huddle for shelter beneath the stairs in their flat.
They began referring to these interludes in cramped quarters during heated times as "baking cakes." Sometimes the
"cakes" would "bake" for days on end. On one occasion
when they were away from home, their kitchen took a direct
hit from a smoldering rocket. Kindly neighbors dragged
away what they could save from the ensuing fire.

Much of the Terrys' work consisted of retrieving
the city's wounded and ferrying them to bare-bones
hospitals across barricades spitting live fire. Fuel for
vehicles, when it was available, cost a fortune. And the
currency of trust, rare to find in good times, was almost
nonexistent in a country at war with itself.

After persevering through years of uncertainty in
Kabul, at the insistence of IAM Dan and Seija eventually

agreed to relocate. In 1996, they and their daughters moved to the northern city of Mazar-i-Sharif, an oasis of relative calm under the iron hand of General Rashid Dostum, a feared, canny Uzbek warlord.

In the course of his community health work, Dan traveled often in the northern backcountry of the storied ruins of Balkh. As sometimes happens in such unsettled times, Dan was captured by a crafty local commander who thought he could spot a windfall when he saw one. Held hostage in the commander's base, Dan assured his captor that there were no riches within reach of any of his friends or family and that threats to his personal health or safety in hopes of ransom would be fruitless.

As the hours passed, the commander observed that Dan was neither anxious nor resentful. They ate together and drank tea as conversation and camaraderie flowered. In time, it dawned on the captor that a strange friendship had sprung up between him and this oddly warm hostage.

Persuaded that any demand for ransom would prove in vain and recognizing in Dan a noble friend, the commander called for a sheep to be slaughtered. A kebab meal sealed the bonds of affection between them. And with that, the commander set him free.

Many months later, when Dan and some of his coworkers were driving through remote country, their Jeep trailing its habitual plume of dust, an open truck full of turbaned gunmen approached from the opposite direction. As the vehicles passed each other, Dan glimpsed at the wheel of the truck the very commander who had once taken him hostage. At the same time, the commander recognized Dantri, the strange foreigner he had taken captive, and both vehicles slid to a stop. Engulfed in dust, the drivers exuberantly embraced with shouts and great claps on the back. They inquired after each other's families, health, and welfare. Gazing down on this improbable scene from the open truck were the commander's fighters, bristling with weapons and bandoliers and bewildered by the sight of their fierce leader in the arms of an infidel. In the Jeep sat Dan's similarly incredulous coworkers, who lived in fear of encountering just such armed rogues.

Experience convinced Dan that nothing precluded trust or understanding, even with those who sometimes wished him ill. He believed that there was no reason to regard the menace of a captor as anything but friendship in disguise.

Experiences such as these crystalized one of the sayings for which Dan was notorious among his coworkers, who could hardly believe their ears whenever he insisted, "Hostage-taking is just another form of hospitality."

III

No one who has yet to ride the long-distance trucks and buses of Afghanistan can say that he or she has fully experienced the country. The mountains readily humble vehicles built for comfort—their rocky tracks tearing out all pretense and sophistication from cars and trucks not engineered for such terrain. All that survive are frames of solid steel and diesel engines that snarl at trouble. Should travelers retain any illusion of ease or comfort, it will vanish at the sight of derelict Soviet-era tanks marking the way, their gun barrels pointing blankly at distant horizons.

For the passengers and cargo in the hands of intrepid Afghan drivers, each journey is a wager from beginning to end. But such road conditions look positively pleasant when compared to the odds of getting past the Kalashnikovs at roadblocks in times of civil war. In 1996, when the Terry family set out by bus from Kabul in hopes of finding a home in Mazar-i-Sharif, they rode straight into the teeth of just such odds.

For the move, Dan had reserved the entire roof-top luggage rack of a public bus for the family's household gear. Like some vision from the American Dust Bowl era, the bus lumbered along, crowned by the skeletons of a previous life: desks, tables, chairs, wardrobes, and other belongings lashed together helter-skelter. Wearing traditional attire, the Terry family had taken their places on the bus with Afghan neighbors, breathing private prayers for heaven's mercy along the way.

On the northward trek, the bus negotiated the warlord roadblocks one by one. At each roadblock, gunmen swaggered onto the bus, barked commands, extorting what they could from compliant passengers. Survival rules are simple: sit at the back with head down, avoid eye contact, and keep silent.

Few passengers were prepared, though, for the brutality that awaited them at one roadblock. The driver's assistant, obviously still an apprentice at this edgy business, somehow attracted the ire of a gunman. Flaring words gave way to a beating with a rifle butt. As the passengers shrank in fear from what must surely follow, Dan stood to his feet in the crowded bus and began taking photographs. The gunman immediately stopped the beating as he and his comrades fastened their attention on the impudent foreigner documenting their behavior. They stormed back to Dan's corner of the bus, shouting curses, and ripping the camera from his hands.

Feigning innocence, Dan apologized, assuring them that they were welcome to take the offending roll of film as guarantee that they would not be incriminated. And then, ever so naturally, he swung his arm firmly around the gunman's bandolier and shoulder in a strong embrace and said, "My brother, the camera is mine." With that, he gently reached over and retrieved it with a broad smile. The slightly unnerved comrades-in-arms retreated, clutching the spent film, and waved the bus with its odd passenger on its way.

Some of those who witnessed this encounter still cluck their tongues to think that a foreigner could have been so naïve as to provoke such an incident. "He should have known that his camera would rile the gunmen," they say. But Dan was far too savvy to think that either he or his camera would escape notice. Rather, in the heat of the violent encounter, he could not sit idly by as cruelty ran its grim course; he intentionally drew the attention of the bullies to himself and away from their Afghan victim in the best way he knew how.

The bus to Mazar-i-Sharif ran a gauntlet of all kinds of dangers that day. But in his surprise gesture, Dan deflected the logic of the gun, took a gamble on peace, and won.

IV

The Terrys' northward shift from Kabul to Mazar-i-Sharif meant mastering new geography, building new networks, and forging new partnerships in an altered ethnic mix that included Tajiks and Uzbeks as well as Hazaras. But Dan and Seija had garnered hard-won wisdom from their years in central Afghanistan. They knew that providing conventional relief or aid as a vision for local development, while sometimes necessary in times of calamity, failed as a long-term approach to bettering the lives of ordinary communities. Far from building up the creative capacities of people, well-meaning outsiders who provided "help" could actually sap a community's dignity and beggar its spirit. The alternative—encouraging a community to find its own voice, articulate its aspirations, and build on its own gifts and strengths—required patient engagement and often restraint. But the results of such a vision could be telling, even inspiring.

As was his penchant, Dan set out to interact with communities that others passed up or neglected. He learned of an isolated settlement that by one account had been neglected "for centuries": a village called Bekh whose inhabitants were largely Ismailis, one of Afghanistan's most disadvantaged religious minorities. Dan and a team of a dozen workers set out to get acquainted with the people and discover whether or not the village had any interest in a partnership to seek a better future.

The mandatory and courtly rituals of welcome, greeting, and inquiries after each other's welfare having been faithfully attended to, conversation turned to the purpose of the visit. The team members expressed interest in learning about Bekh's history and circumstances and tried to draw out the Ismaili elders, wondering what aspirations they might have for the future of their people.

A protracted silence followed as the elders looked blankly at each other. No doubt there was a touch of suspicion about the motives of these visitors; no one had ever asked them such questions or expressed interest in their welfare before. In its forgotten corner, the community had lapsed into acceptance of its neglected state as its unalterable lot. The conversation came to rest at this stage, and the two sides agreed that the visitors would return again later to allow time for further community reflection before resuming dialogue.

At the next visit, with a clear community agenda still absent, the people of Bekh and Dan's team agreed that they would collaborate on an effort to improve basic hygiene. With guidance, the settlement carved nearly 180 septic toilets and bath facilities out of the rocky terrain. Now there were daily reminders of what partnership could produce.

On their third visit, the team resumed conversation with the villagers. This time, the elders' uncertainty was overtaken by a spirited young girl, who rose to say, "We need a school." Her simple comment became the awakening and rallying point for the Ismaili settlement of Bekh. A plan soon followed that enabled the people to build two schools, one for girls and one for boys.

Years passed. The Taliban eventually established their hold over the village. The teachers drifted away for want of support and salary. Much later, an Australian member of that visiting team returned to learn what had become of the Ismailis of Bekh. He found what patience and wisdom could produce in remote and dust-blown lands. Although the trained teachers had long since departed, the schools were still alive. After completing the six years of study available to her in the village, the young Ismaili girl whose voice had galvanized the community had stepped into the role of teacher and flourishing young leader.

V

Dan's drive to know the yonder of Afghan life led him more than once into the shadows. He seemed to follow in the footsteps of the fifth-century Nestorians, who wandered the obscurest corners of mountainous Asia and the Orient with what one chronicler calls "hearts like lions and innocent as doves." Mountain challenges and a gospel calling produced in Dan courage beyond guile.

A story from the reign of the Taliban illustrates Dan's fearlessness. One day he discovered that he had unwittingly allowed his Afghan visa to expire. Dan was never very deft at crossing the official t's or dotting the requisite i's, though he compensated by mastering the art of sincere praise. He presented himself at the foreigners' registration bureau with an air of contrition, only to be told that a new law now required offenders to spend a day in jail for every day of infraction. He had been in violation of the law for thirty days.

Dan was not the first foreigner to have accidentally violated such regulations. The usual way of handling such incidents was to prevail upon some broker or influential friend to intercede with a senior official, who would then dismiss the offense with a stern warning. But to the disquiet of his friends and colleagues, Dan declined to finesse his way out of trouble. To those who sought to reason with him, who counseled that it would be foolhardy or even dangerous to be held in a Taliban prison, Dan replied, "Time in prison will not be wasted time." This was his chance to make acquaintance with the disgraced who languished in the shadows of the Taliban regime. "There are people in prison I should know," he said to the consternation of his more measured friends.

The wardens and inmates in the Kabul jail could hardly believe that a hapless foreigner had landed in their midst, but it was not long before they discovered this was no clueless traveler. With gentle heart, Dantri immersed himself in the accounts of misfortune that had brought the inmates, most of them Hazaras, to such degrading conditions. He was witness to the things they suffered: deprivation, cable beatings, lice, interrogations, and humiliation. He later recalled that a cup of greasy, fried onions offered to him in prison was the best meal he had ever had.

At one point, a Taliban informant posing as a prisoner was sent to listen to the loose, incriminating talk that prison boredom produces and perhaps to collect further evidence against Dan. But it was not in Dan's nature to insult others, however easy or tempting the target. He had mastered the discipline of being a gracious guest even in revolting conditions—even in prison. When Dan's family and friends brought food, clothing, blankets, or medicine to the prison, the supplies became the common property of all the inmates, some of whom were ill and in states of serious neglect.

At one point, the warden of the prison—nervous, perhaps, that something grave might befall this foreigner while in his custody—told him to go home, that by his rough calculation Dan had served sufficient time. Happy for an early release, Dan went home, had a warm shower, sat in his customary place at the table with his family, and slept in his own bed.

The next day there was a knock at the door. It was the Taliban police. They apologized profusely, informing Dan that there had been an error and that, on recalculation, he had additional days yet to serve in prison. They sheepishly asked if he would kindly accompany them back to detention. As someone who understood that mistakes in math are common to us all, Dan cheerfully gathered his things and went with his chagrined chaperones back to prison.

Had Dan's fellow inmates been granted release from prison, they surely would have recognized it as an opportunity to abscond. They were thunderstruck when, twenty-four hours later, Dan quite willingly marched up to the prison gates to resume his sentence. One witness describes how this news brought the disbelieving inmates swarming out into the prison yard, where they watched the gates swing open to take Dantri back. They broke into spontaneous cheers and applause over the return of this rare and congenial foreigner.

A watchman outside Dan's workplace in Kabul reported that sometimes in the following years furtive strangers would drift along the street and pause to inquire if this was the place where Dantri worked. "Yes," the guard would tell them. "Shall I call him for you?' "No," they would reply. "We once met him in prison, and he befriended us there."

Dan refused to regard any of this as particularly unusual and later offered the following bit of hard-earned wisdom: If ever you want to become fluent in another language, get yourself sentenced to some serious prison time.

VI

If Dan had endeared himself to local communities with his humor, courtly deference, and honor, they also trusted him because of his curiosity about all things Afghan: idiomatic language, traditional wisdom and mores, families and names, ethnic distinctives, and deep history.

An Afghan colleague tells of an encounter between Dan and a Pashtun from Kandahar, the spiritual home of the Taliban. Dan wondered what part of the city the Pashtun called home. He replied that he lived in a quarter next to a certain Muslim shrine. Always looking for fun, Dan asked the man if he remembered how many steps there were leading up to that very shrine. Caught off guard at this unexpected question, the man responded that there were many but that he had never counted them. To the amazement of the man and bystanders, Dan answered his own question: "There are forty steps!" Only a penitent pilgrim or extra-ordinarily observant visitor could have numbered and remembered each of those sacred steps.

Dan's curiosity about the lives of Afghans and their families led him to form unusually strong bonds with ordinary people. There is the story of Dan and Seija's encounter with a family whose mother had cared for an invalid husband. He had been felled by osteomyelitis in the knees, in the very region where Dan and his medical colleagues would later have a fateful encounter that would make them page-one news.

Invited to the family home, Dan came face to face with the stark reality faced by so many Afghans. The father lay in the last agonies of tuberculosis, with opium the only medicine to ease the pain. The entire local community, who knew well the helplessness of the family, witnessed Dan's visit and likely wondered what difference this foreigner might make. Dan and others began clearing a long-neglected nearby airstrip. Using sagebrush cut from the valley as brooms, they swept away the many years of accumulated debris. Then, to the amazement of the hamlet, a small Cessna arrived to take the patient and his wife to Kabul for palliative care.

Though the man's death could not be averted, the families were now forever fused in friendship. The man's family bonded with Dan and with Seija, who had received them at the hospital in Kabul and arranged for their care. In ensuing years, the family members would call Dan and Seija on a borrowed satellite phone, inquiring after their health and sharing news of their neighbors. Although his natural curiosity may have led Dan into sharing the grief and loss of a distant family, his humanity made him and Seija their next-of-kin.

VII

In later years, when Dan and Seija returned periodically to North America to reconnect with family, friends, and church communities, their message and demeanor spoke powerfully of how the reality they experienced in Afghanistan was at variance with the caricatures known to the larger world. In particular, their witness challenged the view propagated by mainstream news that members and supporters of the Taliban were beyond the civilized pale or even demonic.

By the late 1990s, accounts of the Taliban's extreme social code had already won an established place in media reports. Dan and Seija readily admitted the sufferings associated with the strictures of the Taliban code, but they also described the working relationships they had with local Taliban authorities, who sought the welfare of their communities and had proven to be worthy partners in shared endeavors. To the astonishment of his American audience, Dan frequently asserted that he counted Taliban commanders among his friends.

Dan would offer the following account to his skeptical hearers: At a particularly difficult time during the closing months of Taliban rule in mid-2001, foreign humanitarian groups and particularly Christian agencies had fallen under hostile scrutiny by the authorities. One day on his way home to his place of assignment at Lal wa Sar Jangal, Dan stopped to have tea with the local Taliban commander in the area's administrative center. They visited congenially, chatting about family and health and the prospect of harvest.

Finally Dan rose to leave, explaining that he needed to arrive home before nightfall. The commander raised his hand to indicate that there was just one more thing he needed to say; he had received a directive from his superiors to detain Dan for interrogation in Kabul. But as it happened, the commander explained, he faced a considerable backlog of work and would not be able to execute the directive for about thirty-six hours. And what is more, he admitted, with a light in his eyes, he was shorthanded and would not be able to patrol the roads and highways until further notice.

The message was clear: the commander found it unconscionable to take his neighbor and friend into custody, and he was begging Dan to be absent when he came to perform his unpleasant duty. Dan gladly obliged. He went home, packed up his Jeep, and vanished with Seija, crossing the mountains into Pakistan.

3

The Dantri Road

I

The Hazara people of central Afghanistan know the backhand of fate. Neither geography nor history has been kind to them. At the best of times, the living they wrest from their slopes and narrow valleys is a hardscrabble business. Living at the convergence of empires—ruled in turn by the Greeks, Persians, Mongols, Indians, Russians, and British—they look askance at ambitious neighbors under whose boot they have sometimes suffered. The elders require little encouragement to recite their litany of massacres: 1856, 1892, 1998, and 2001.

Six-month winters have schooled the Hazaras in resilience and resourcefulness, but when the harvests fail and the pastures wither for a year or two, these proud people trudge away from their flinty homeland in search of survival elsewhere—anywhere. Today they are scattered not only in large cities such as Kabul and Mazar-i-Sharif but also beyond, in Iran, Pakistan, and as far as India.

It was this history of enduring hardship and the fortitude it has produced that first drew Dan to Hazarajat, the central highland region the Hazaras call home. After years in Kabul and then Mazar-i-Sharif, circumstances in 1998 called him back to Lal wa Sar Jangal, the community he had first loved and served. From Lal wa Sar Jangal, Dan could see that a secure future for the Hazaras depended on their ability to link together their many grassroots community groups for joint endeavor and as a bulwark against trouble. This regional network—including councils of elders, women's groups, health cooperatives, and a variety of local development agencies—came to be known as *Ertabet*, meaning "contacts."

Drought and winters were not the only adversaries in the region. The Taliban, historically at odds with the Hazara people, had confiscated many of their herds, and rival Koochi herders had been brought in to take over Hazara pastures. In addition, decades of war left deadly mines in their agricultural lands, preventing farmers from working their fields. The few farmers who still had access to land were finding onions and opium poppies more marketable than barley and wheat.

In 1999, a hunger belt emerged in Hazarajat. The Ertabet network monitored the local conditions, telegraphing the approaching calamity. What started as a thin trickle became a steady flow of Hazaras leaving their valley homes. Households in outlying areas increasingly resorted to famine foods from the wild. Traditional users of tobacco, no longer able to afford their habit, took up sucking on *kaf* (seeds of dockleaf) to ease their cravings. The most vulnerable groups—infants, children, and mothers—exhibited troubling signs of malnutrition.

As the famine emerged ever more insistently, Dan vowed to a friend, "All I want is to keep the Hazaras from becoming refugees in their own country." But remedies remained a long arm's length away. By 1999, the Taliban had earned the mistrust of the international community, which was not inclined to be generous with a pariah state. In addition, internal divisions between Afghans were deep and bitter, and front lines of open conflict obstructed potential supply lines. The traditional enmity between the largely Pashtun Taliban and the Hazaras made mounting any effective relief effort a long shot.

But a signature trait of Dan's work was the formation of unlikely yet effective partnerships. One of his friends, Shahir Zahine, a Pashtun businessman with Taliban contacts and experience in humanitarian work, secured the acquiescence of the Taliban administration in Kabul to a plan for bringing relief to the Hazaras. Michael Semple and Mervyn Patterson, experienced regional humanitarian workers, took on the sensitive diplomatic mission of winning the approval of senior Taliban figures in Kandahar. Dan's responsibility was to work out ground-level political and logistical arrangements for the relief trucks to roll into Hazarajat. Meanwhile, the United Nations' World Food Programme and the European Union agreed to provide grain to forestall starvation.

In their approaches to senior Taliban authorities, Semple, Patterson, and Zahine discovered what the mass media in the West have failed to communicate: though the Taliban are responsible for many outrages, they at times worked willingly for the good of the Afghan people. Indeed, the Taliban administration in Kabul was prepared not only to grant permission for the relief supplies to be sent to the Hazaras but also to provide modest resources to make the scheme feasible. A senior Taliban official in Kandahar observed flatly, "They [the Hazaras] are Afghans too."

The race was on to save Hazara communities entombed by winter conditions. The roads into the Hazara homeland had never in living memory been passable in winter, but Dan was convinced it could be done if communities worked together. With the Ertabet network buzzing and a food-for-work scheme in hand, Dan went in search of the trucks and drivers capable of facing the daunting road conditions. Blacksmiths in the bazaars worked feverishly to produce the snow chains Dan had designed for vehicles, which he hoped would successfully challenge the mountain snowdrifts and frozen rivers.

The truck routes into the mountains passed through areas of uncertain control. Though Hazara armed resistance to Taliban encroachment had largely collapsed, Taliban enmity against the Hazaras still smoldered, and official Taliban backing for the enterprise in Kabul and Kandahar did not guarantee unhindered passage on the ground. Dan used his persuasive powers with factional groups by "enfranchising" them—one of his favorite terms—by making them partners in the design and execution of the relief plan. The ultimate incentive was that Taliban families and their sympathizers who lived in the central highlands would also be spared the scourge of hunger.

After a chain of tea-sweetened agreements was cobbled together, armies of villagers turned out with shovels and picks to do battle not with their ethnic enemies but with snow and ice. They accomplished what no generation of Hazaras had seen before: open winter roads. At the same time, convoys loaded with bags of grain wound their way out of Kabul and into the silent backcountry hills. Crowds of hungry and astonished Hazaras gathered to applaud the first-ever sight. When the vehicles could go no further, donkey caravans were pressed into service, and beyond that, able-bodied men walked the life-saving grain into the snow-drifted mountain villages.

As this drama of deliverance played out, Dan resembled a mad dervish: now under the hood of a balky vehicle, now indistinguishable in a crew at work on a mountainous snowdrift, now barking on

Crews of Hazaras labor to clear drifts of snow from what came to be known as the "Dantri Road" for winter delivery of life-saving wheat in 1999. Photograph by Dan Terry.

the phone to secure diesel fuel, now striding through a snowfield to test a route, now fastening chains on a truck, now arguing with a troublesome official, now pressing a hesitant driver to run a gauntlet of ice, now laying his hand upon some child to say that food was coming.

One of the Afghans who worked with him on this effort recalled, "It seemed so foolhardy, but we felt ashamed that an outsider would outdo us in the desperate race to save Hazara lives. He was the first into the frigid rivers to dislodge stalled vehicles and the last to climb up out of the mud after repairs on a breakdown." Another devout Afghan friend reflected, "When Dantri worked day and night to save the Hazaras from famine, he showed that he was more Muslim than the Muslims."

At one stage, as four trucks labored through an agricultural area, the convoy had to leave an impassable section of road and cross an adjoining grain field. Seeing his crop damaged, the farmer challenged the last truck, beating its driver with the butt of his rifle. Noticing trouble, Dan swung down out of his vehicle and walked back to the enraged farmer and bloodied driver. He offered heartfelt regrets, accepted full responsibility for the damage, and then pleaded with the farmer to join him in doing whatever was necessary to save Hazara lives. When the empty trucks returned, the farmer warmly received Dantri, shared a celebratory cup of tea with him, and posed with him and the driver for a photograph that sealed friendship in the face of hunger.

Another driver recalled a particularly slippery route they traversed late one night:

> Our loaded truck brought us to a steep grade already badly rutted with mud everywhere. We made several attempts to climb the slope, but failed each time. It was near midnight, and we could see that darkness and the road conditions would get the best of us. Sensing defeat, we sat silently, each with our own thoughts. Then Dantri said, "Shut down the engine. We will sleep a short while. I think I know how we can get through."
>
> We huddled together in the cab for warmth, wondering what Dantri had in mind. Some hours later, while it was still dark, Dantri got out to walk the road. "We can go now," he said, as he climbed back into the cab. I eased the truck up the road, fully expecting to see us mire down with such a heavy load. But no, the truck powered past the ruts, up the incline that brought us safely to the pass. Dantri had realized that if we were patient, the winter cold would eventually take hold, freezing the muddy stretches and providing the traction we needed to get the food through. The bitter cold was the Hazaras' friend that night.

Reflecting on the Hazara operation as a whole, Michael Semple observed,

> That whole effort was excellent value for money. The donor agencies have rarely had such an effective and efficient effort. By contrast, the parallel attempt to push relief food into the Panjshir Valley held by Ahmed Shah Mehsoud, a hero of the resistance to the Soviets, was dogged with dramas and inefficiencies. For that reason, it received

extensive coverage in the world press. But the
Hazara operation received hardly any mention at
all because it went so smoothly.

All told, 380 truckloads, each carrying twelve
tons of wheat, threaded their way through the political brambles, traversed the front lines of conflict, and
conquered the Afghan winter to fend off the scythe of
hunger. About twenty truckloads were hijacked at gun-
point and lost to armed groups.

When the Hazara communities emerged alive from
their winter cocoon, they had a name for the once-in-a-
lifetime truck route that had brought them succor: the
"Dantri Road."

II

Although he was scrupulously principled in his personal dealings, Dan did have his excesses. He carried
on a determined love affair with machines, preferably
machines with wheels. He was especially vulnerable to
anything with outsized knobby tires that could take on
mountain scree like high-end hiking boots.

Dan seemed to have acquired his innate savvy about
things mechanical from his father. The rest of what he
knew about their care and design was learned on the fly
or behind the family woodshed. For someone who had
hardly any acquisitive impulse, Dan cared altogether
too tenderly for a succession of four-wheel-drive vehicles: Land Rovers, Toyota Land Cruisers, and German
Unimogs. But the apple of his roustabout eye was a
World War II–era CJ-2 Willys Jeep that he acquired in
murky circumstances and sheltered in the West Virginia
hills. Given his long absences in the Hindu Kush, Dan
had a visiting relationship with this Jeep. She was his
kept creature.

Today, in a shaded courtyard in Kabul, there
remains another telling artifact of Dan's runaway fascination for machines that might match the mountains

of Afghanistan. The vehicle is an odd medley of parts. Over the years, Dan observed how different vehicles withstood the punishment of the backcountry. None had all the winning components, so he began to marry the proven features of various vehicles in a quest for a super-machine. The result is the "Afghan Jeep": a hybrid machine consisting of a Russian cab, a Toyota engine and chassis, and parts cribbed from many other vehicles. The cab roof has been ripped off and raised willy-nilly to accommodate Dan's six-foot frame. It bears the telltale fingerprints of both its inventor's hand and the harsh terrain that is its native home.

An Afghan friend recalls the day he and Dantri went to register this vehicle with the transport authorities. "The clerks were utterly bewildered," he recounts.

> They had no idea how to complete the required forms. We drank tea as they scratched their heads and furrowed their foreheads, since it fit none of the usual categories. It was partly this and partly that. We still do not know what they wrote in their book. But to us, it is the "Afghan Jeep," which exists in no other country.

Indeed, the Afghan Jeep has now passed—like the elusive *barmanu*[1]—into the lore of the Hindu Kush.

No mountain-worthy vehicle of Dan's would be equal to Himalayan challenges without an accompanying bag of tricks. In the courtyard near the Afghan Jeep is an assortment of tackle and winches, reserve supplies, and tools. For example, years of battling snowdrifts in Hazara country had yielded ingeniously designed, locally made chains. Perhaps most intriguing are what look like two metal ramps behind a storage shed: aluminum cross-sections of airplane wings, whose sturdy interior construction and light weight make them perfect for throwing across washouts or off-road ravines.

---

1. *Barmanu*: Afghanistan's version of the yeti, or Bigfoot

Dan would strap them onto the Afghan Jeep at the outset of any journey. Taken together, the Jeep and its accoutrements are reminiscent of an earlier Terry vehicle that his father had cobbled together and that had traversed these very mountain roads thirty years before.

Dan's affections were not limited to four-wheeled machines. He also owned a mountain bike he called "Precious." It, too, was a unique hybrid, part Chinese and part American. His affection for this sturdy conveyance, which took him down the alleyways of Kabul and on winter traverses of the mountains, was forever sealed the day he rode up to an army checkpoint. An argument was underway involving a taxi driver and a hothead soldier. Some scuffling ensued, followed by inadvertent gunshots from the soldier's rifle. When it was all over, Dan—a bystander to the confusion—stood trying to reason with the clumsy soldier while blood pooled at his feet. His Reeboks were turning crimson. A stray bullet had ricocheted off Precious's handlebars and pierced Dan's thigh.

Someone called an ambulance and bystanders helped Dan aboard. But before he could be whisked away, Dan insisted that he would not leave Precious behind; after all, she too had been wounded. The bicycle was trundled into the ambulance, and they sped away to urgent care. When Dan was taken into surgery, he reportedly refused all care until Precious was wheeled into the operating theater where he could keep her under his possessive eye.

A redeeming detail brings to a close this tragicomic roadside incident. Later that day a soldier who had been present at the mishap suffered an injury in another altercation. Brought to the same hospital, he ended up in the bed beside Dan's, and both recognized the improbable opportunity for reconciliation. Days of side-by-side therapy and stories fortified with the laughter of brothers who have shared the folly and hard

knocks of war cemented their bond. When released
from the hospital, Dan with his bike and the soldier
with his rifle, they could not part as anything but kin.
Reflecting on this episode, Dan said, "I am now a true
Afghan because I have eaten with them bread, salt, and
now shrapnel."

III

Dan's instinct was to set his feet on ground that others
rarely if ever walked. His ruling curiosity often took
him down less-traveled roads and into country seldom
seen by outsiders.

A companion recounts how once, while driving a
familiar highway, Dan noticed a newly opened side-
track. Since the road was still under construction, a
barrier had been erected, forbidding entry. Though facing time constraints, Dan reversed his orange all-terrain
Unimog and gazed down the rugged trace leading away
into the hills. The unknown was just too tantalizing to
pass up. He climbed out of the truck and dragged the
barrier to one side, then turned the nose of the vehicle
toward whatever lay beyond their range of vision.

Dan (not visible) and fellow travelers stop to assist the first truck of the season arriving in a remote valley. "Precious," Dan's fabled bike, is lashed to the roof of the 4x4.
Photograph by Dan Jantzen, used with permission.

Dan's colleague cleared his throat in hesitation, then suggested that maybe the barrier had been erected for good reason: hazards to the vehicle, body, or even soul might await them. But Dan waved off the reluctance with a grin and delivered a trademark "Dan-ism": "You never know when a side road might come in handy."

Rough country and a rude grade brought them to a mountain saddle beyond which silent ranks of ridges marched away as far as the eye could see. They stood for a while, taking in the drama of such a majestic land. Against the whistle of the wind, his colleague heard Dan murmur, "The last outsiders to stand here were Marco Polo and his party."

Dan's fascination for trails into the yonder of the mountains once led him down a freshly cut track that brought him to a party of young men working with picks and shovels to wrest a road from the wilderness. Having never ventured beyond their remote mountain area, the young men gazed in amazement upon Dan's snarling, wheeled machine—the likes of which they had never seen.

Since their village was nearby, the young men invited Dantri and the vehicle to their settlement, where he enjoyed the obligatory tea and repartee with elders and curious bystanders. As evening crept over the hills, Dan begged his leave to retrace his route and resume the journey. When he returned to the truck, a strange sight awaited him. There, by the front bumper of the vehicle, was a small mound of hay. This remote but exquisitely hospitable people had provided forage for the creature that would, with great exertion, bear him home.

IV

Traveling one day after a rain, Dan and an Afghan colleague approached a mountain settlement by vehicle. Along the highway, two boys had seized the opportunity to create their own little village from the road's fresh mud. Hunched happily over their work, they hardly noticed the car approaching them. But Dan noticed them. He reached over to tell his driver friend to throttle back. As they neared the boys, Dan asked him to leave a wide berth so as not to endanger the boys' creation and then requested the driver to stop. He got out and squatted beside the two surprised boys. A roadside chat ensued, with the children proudly pointing out to Dan the features of their creation.

After a time, Dan said goodbye and climbed back into the car, his hands still grimy with the roadside mud from which a playful world was being carefully—and peaceably—fashioned.

On another occasion, Dan and a friend passed through a small settlement on motorcycle. As they passed the adobe homes, a menacing Afghan wolfhound came howling out to the road, announcing his sovereignty in those parts. Dan stopped the cycle, dismounted, and raced directly at the hound, waving his arms and shrieking like a demon. No such challenge had ever before been issued to the village hound. It lost its composure, turned, and ran yelping for cover.

That evening, as Dan mused with his companion about their travels, he voiced regret at the incident with the hound. "That poor dog," said Dan, "I humiliated it before its entire village!"

V

Few people would want to be called by the name *Pagal* ("Crazy"), which occurs in many South Asian languages. But it is a name that settled quite securely on Dan, a name by which he was widely and affectionately known around Afghanistan and which he readily accepted and even seemed to revel in. That "crazy" side of Dan resonated powerfully with a broad and whimsical streak in local lore. Afghans love to recount the tales of Mullah Nasruddin, a wacky but loveable figure of legend who is at once witty, wise, and impossibly naïve. Mullah Nasruddin sometimes rides his donkey backwards and might be seen standing on his head in the bazaar for no apparent reason.

To some, Dan was *Pagal* because of his nonchalance in the face of danger and hardship. At a particularly unsettled time, when Dan had taken refuge in Kabul because of uncertainty in the provinces, he planned a road trip back to Lal wa Sar Jangal, the community where he had worked among the Hazara people. An Afghan friend insisted that he should go along to smooth the way and keep him company.

"No," replied Dan. "You will only cry there. Food and tea you won't find. Only crusts of dry *naan*.[2] Here you can remain at peace with your family. I go only because I am *Pagal*. That is why I am drawn to dangerous places."

On another occasion, Dan was standing in his courtyard in Kabul visiting with a guest, who observed that the tree whose shade they were enjoying had become a hazard. "This tree will soon bring thieves into your home," warned the guest. "They will climb into its branches, pass over your wall, and steal everything you have. You'd better cut it down before you become a victim of crime."

"No," Dan answered the visitor. "I do not fear thieves."

"Then at least get a guard dog," urged the friend.

"Why do I need a dog?" shrugged Dan, the *Pagal*. "God's protection is enough for me."

At other times, Dan, like the fabled Mullah Nasruddin, was composed in the face of insults and provocations. A companion remembers coming to a roadblock in northern Afghanistan, where four surly

2. *Naan*: an oven-baked flatbread

commanders made no secret of their intention to confiscate Dan's Afghan Jeep. They shouted demeaning names and insisted that he must be from the despised United Nations, which had often tried to call regional militias to account for their human rights abuses.

A young boy standing nearby interjected, "No, he could not be from the UN. I have seen him in the bazaar in Mazar-i-Sharif. He is the one they call *Pagal*." For this telling bit of information, the boy was rewarded by a swat with the butt of a rifle. But the commanders had lost their swagger, and Dan slipped through the opening created by the boy. "Let me explain," he said in Dari. "The boy is right. I do live in Mazar-i-Sharif, and it is my work to serve the people." Soon Dan could be seen in a roadside tête-à-tête, his arms around the shoulders of the commanders. They had been won over by a stranger who had fully earned the local name, *Pagal*.

Sometimes people thought that Dan was slightly unhinged, because he insisted on the good in all people, often in the face of overwhelming evidence to the contrary. During the Hazara famine, an Afghan coworker complained bitterly to Dan about a young man on a road crew who had an "unfriendly air" and worked in sullen silence. "Let's get rid of him now," pleaded the foreman, "before he poisons the whole crew with his attitude."

"No," counseled Dan. "Haven't you noticed how he refrains from flattery? And he works as hard as any of them. That is good." By the end of the road-building project the foreman had to concede that Dan had been right. The apparently troubled man had established himself as a trusted crew leader.

In some of these stories about Dantri the *Pagal*, there are actual echoes of lines from Mullah Nasruddin tales. A friend once saw Dan carrying his fabled mountain bike, Precious, on his shoulder as he walked through the Kabul bazaar. Bystanders began to laugh and indulge in some good-natured ribbing. "Why is it," rejoined Dantri with a wry smile, "that when my long-suffering bike carries me every day, I never hear you laugh? But when I, for once, carry my bike, you cannot contain your glee?" This comment was greeted with hoots of delight from the bazaar-goers, who remembered tales of Mullah Nasruddin carrying his donkey.

In other instances it was Dan's uncanny instincts that lent him the air of *Pagal*. Driving once through unfamiliar country toward dusk, Dan's party of travelers completely lost their bearings. Hour after pitch-black hour Dan drove on through rugged terrain, much to the anxiety of his passengers, who had now resigned themselves to a sorry fate in uncertain country.

At one o'clock in the morning their headlights fell upon an inn at the edge of the very village they had been seeking. The scant servings of cold rice served up for supper seemed to the travelers a feast in their astonishment at having arrived precisely where they intended to be. Dan's wit and audacity in successfully navigating through darkness, mountains, and rivers could only be ascribed to *Pagal*—certainly not to a human being in possession of normal faculties.

Sometimes that craziness, that audacity, left Dan's companions—and even him—breathless and weak-kneed. During the years that Dan and Seija lived in Mazar-i-Sharif, they were sometimes called on to provide urgently needed supplies to those working in rural communities. A message arrived one day that gasoline had run out at a critical point and that resupply was desperately required. Dan secured the fuel in fifty-five-gallon drums and asked an Afghan coworker to deliver it. But beyond the edge of town, the driver came to a roadblock. The local warlord, Rashid Dostum, had issued an order that in light of tight supplies no one was to take gasoline out of the city. Reprimanded and turned back by the soldiers, the driver reported to Dan that he could not deliver the fuel.

Knowing how much hinged upon the arrival of this fuel, Dan insisted he would find a way. Taking the wheel of the Jeep himself, he and the coworker approached the city outskirts. His coworker wondered how *Pagal* would finesse this obstacle, which was backed up with Kalashnikovs. As Dan approached the checkpoint, his eyes narrowed. Instead of easing back as the usual protocol required, he floored the accelerator and torpedoed past the astonished and somewhat sleepy soldiers. They did not even have time to grab their rifles to take control of the situation, which had gone seriously *pagal*.

"A kilometer or two down the road, Dantri pulled over and got out," recalls the companion. "He leaned trembling against the Jeep, his head in his hands. We saw a spring by the side of the road where we went to wash our faces, cool ourselves, and recover our senses."

After delivering the fuel to a grateful community, Dan and his coworker crept back into the city under cover of darkness by a circuitous route known to Dan and very few others. Dostum's soldiers may still be wondering what happened that day at the checkpoint. It was their brush with *Pagal*.

The ultimate affirmation of the goodness and appeal of this moniker came when a circle of war-weary Afghans in the central highlands proposed the formation of an informal society around the notion. Not surprisingly, Dantri held office in it for many years. Its name? The *Hezb-i-Pagal*: the "Party of Crazies." The sole condition of membership is a "mad" pledge to seek the good of the community and to disavow fighting and corruption. With a measure of whimsy, it runs counter to a political life often based on religious zealotry or ethnic interest that has yielded only a harvest of suffering.

The Hezb-i-Pagal is now headquartered in the town of Qizil, west of Kabul, and it has recognized leaders. In more recent times the condition for membership includes a first-time donation of two hundred sun-dried bricks to be used for community building. Schools, mosques, and clinics long lying in ruins have reappeared, bringing hope to dispirited settlements where the *pagals* have rallied to dream.

VI

Though Afghans affectionately knew Dan as *Pagal*, he did not always meet with the same humor or acceptance among his Western peers. The story of his ties with the venerable service agency, the International Assistance Mission (IAM), is particularly revealing. Prophets and visionaries of peacemaking bent can only rarely find an enduring home, even in altruistic institutions.

During Dan's early years in the 1970s and 1980s, when he was frequently outside Kabul in the hinterland, his peers found nothing objectionable in his urge to press beyond the conventions of development work. One observer remarks, "Dan seemed a seminal figure in IAM's ethos and culture." His bonding with Afghans, unabashed love of mountain communities, free-spirited courage, and command of language and culture were the very traits IAM sought in its workers. This was also, not incidentally, the period when Dan's father, George—the bolt of cloth from which Dan himself was cut—served as director of IAM.

But IAM was on a growth path of its own: expanding staff, broadening horizons, requiring standardized resource controls, and creating ever more complex management systems. Dan, like his Afghan Jeep, could not easily be cataloged in clerical ledgers; his activities were often "Spirit-led" rather than designed, he was oblivious to the clock, he was often disheveled in organizational matters, and he insisted on prophetic values. All of these attributes made him problematic to a smoothly functioning agency.

A director who had once severely reprimanded him in public later confided to a friend, "He's the loveliest

person I've ever known, but he drives me insane!"
Another remarked, "He was a wonderful friend but a
bewildering colleague." Others observed of Dan that
he had so fully taken on the character of the communities he served, "he was an Afghan trapped in a Western
frame." And perhaps most intriguing of all, one coworker mused, "He brought out the madness in us all."
Illustrating his point, the coworker continued,

> On one occasion, Dan had despaired so com-
> pletely of the way the larger world had approached
> the Taliban that [he suggested] a radically new
> approach should be pioneered. He proposed tak-
> ing a party of families—including women and
> children—straight into Helmand Province, the
> thorniest swath of Taliban country, as a sign of
> sincere friendship. Agency leadership was aghast
> at the administrative complications that would
> ensue from such a naïve gesture. What was even
> more alarming was that five others, persuaded
> of his proposal, volunteered to join Dan in this
> unconventional gambit. But this project was
> never permitted to see the light of day and died
> an early death.

So unsettling did this organizational disquiet
become that Dan was suspected of mental illness—of
being *pagal* in the least congenial sense possible. A condition of his return to work in Afghanistan after one
home leave was that he undergo a psychiatric evalu-
ation at a California clinic. Winning the endorsement
of the clinic, where he was famous for taking residents
on roistering bike outings, Dan was judged to be in
full possession of his faculties and cleared to return to
Afghanistan. That vindication came as cold comfort,
however; by now he was an increasingly marginal-
ized figure among his IAM colleagues, particularly his
superiors.

Dan's project proposals for the central highlands,
his informal work in seeking hostage releases, his

initiatives in rehabilitating drug-addicted youths, and his interventions to mitigate violence amid rising bloodshed—these were met with jaundiced eyes. In time IAM would sever its ties with Dan, who was increasingly seen as a loose cannon and risky to agency coherence and stability.

The onward path for Dan, while still open, narrowed now and led through shadows as he dealt with feelings of betrayal and loneliness. Shaken in self-confidence and deprived of the affirmation of those under whose auspices he had long served, Dan's search for moorings and a framework for his endeavors proved as painful as the sharp complaints from his increasingly arthritic knees. He would later find the support he craved with an organization called Future Generations and with individuals who recognized his gifts.

Meanwhile, IAM suffered losses too. In exchange for tidiness and a measure of organizational control, it lost Dan's community-driven perspective, his prophetic depth of vision, and his creative and infectious passion.

When Dan's IAM coworkers reflect on the growing rift with their former colleague, their words convey wistful soul-searching. How could one so rich in spirit and visionary service have failed to meet with understanding among his peers? How could agency leaders yield to the lure of short-term program harmony and forfeit Dan's rare feel for the pitfalls and promise of community work? And how could one devoted to reconciliation and justice have lost the bridges linking him to his fellow volunteers?

Despite his hardships, Dan's drive to make his gifts and peacemaking impulses useful would not be deflected. As he learned to surmount knee pain and navigate rugged country with his walking stick and bike, he also learned to deal with the handicaps of fading agency support. He pressed doggedly on, working increasingly with those who recognized his grasp of Afghan realities and valued his insights and indomitable hope.

VII

Although he was a product of Western upbringing and had been schooled in upstanding Methodist virtues and orderliness, Dan was incorrigibly tardy. As a schoolboy, he was famous for sliding into class in the middle of attendance roll call; a surname starting with a "T" only just saved him from perpetual after-school detention. In school orchestra practice, the Haydn overture would be well along by the time Dan crept into the trumpet chair, muttering profuse apologies while raising a cold mouthpiece to his lips for the brass solo.

A church leader in north Florida recalls expecting Dan, their guest speaker from the Hindu Kush, on a Sunday morning. The entire congregation waited in suspense, wondering what might have befallen their no-show guest. When he and Seija finally arrived, much to the relief of the worship leaders, Dan explained to the congregation, "It is one thing to navigate the trackless Himalaya; it is quite another to find the way along American interstates, I assure you!" Another Florida friend laughs as he recalls taking off his own watch and strapping it to Dan's wrist in recognition that American Methodists—not to mention airlines—tend to be less forgiving in matters of punctuality than the Hazaras.

More businesslike colleagues failed to see any charm in this flaw. Their frustration at working with Dan was only sharpened with setbacks to their own work plans or schedules on account of his tardiness. But even in the unpleasant consequences of Dan's life-long lateness, there were sometimes signs of strength.

A visiting foundation executive recalls traveling in Dan's company for several days in post-Taliban times. Dan's insistence on taking several byroads of discovery had resulted in a full day's delay in the visitor's schedule. On the visitor's last day in the country, they dashed for the Pakistan-Afghanistan border as light was fading and the gate was due to close. Arriving at the border crossing at the Khyber Pass, the party was greeted by a locked barrier with closed offices and soldiers and immigration officials preparing to leave. Waiting until morning would mean the visitor would miss his onward itinerary out of Peshawar.

Waiting under the canopy of a nearby tree, the anxious visitor watched as Dan set to work. As most Afghans do, Dan believed that virtually everything could be negotiated. Nothing this side of heaven could be hard and fast. First, it was necessary to grasp the topography of authority and then to deftly apply the resources of culture and language. "It was like some elegant dance," the visitor recalls. An arabesque of plea and contrition here, a pirouette of proverb there, a downcast gaze for shame of failed hospitality over yonder. Dan's masterful choreography, and the sympathies of officials, turned the key.

Contrary to all regulations, with darkness fallen and the hour long passed, the gate swung open as the rifle-slung guards and ink-stained bureaucrats who had greeted them with stony disdain wished them "*Salaam aleikum*"—"Peace be with you"—for their onward journey.

Only a handful of people know how to pick that lock, says the visitor.

VIII

If Dan's resolve and daring as a peacemaker sometimes made him seem heroic, the testimonies of his colleagues restore his full humanity. Conflict with peers—particularly his Western compatriots—followed him doggedly.

Years of work in Lal wa Sar Jangal ended painfully in the late 1990s, with Dan coming under personal criticism from fellow volunteers for having fashioned a working relationship with patriarchal Taliban authorities. In other cases, he so passionately took the part of Afghans in debates about program direction, he forfeited the trust of some of his foreign coworkers.

After the winter famine among the Hazaras, Dan was pilloried by donor agency staff members whose paperwork and standard operating procedures had fallen by the wayside in the snowdrifts and frozen rivers of Bamian. That some would question his personal integrity—the currency that underwrote so much of his work and his only shield when the bullets started flying—stung him deeply. These barbs and his growing estrangement from his home agency, IAM, made Dan's family bonds even more critical to his inner strength.

A story from later years captures Dan's growing personal complexities. In time, Dan and Seija's daughters made their way one by one back to the United States for university studies. Hilja, the eldest, and her sister Anneli found a second home with a welcoming town doctor and his wife in Amherst, Massachusetts. The entire Terry clan gathered there eventually for Hilja's wedding. On the eve of the ceremony, Dan found some time to walk the surrounding hills to clear his mind and be refreshed. When he returned from the day's ramble, he was unusually quiet. The host, a physician, wanted to be sure Dan was not ill. Though Dan first brushed off his inquiries, he finally admitted that he had fallen during his walk and had bruised his hand, which was now painfully swollen. This turned out to be much more than a bruise; his hand was broken and required a cast.

At the wedding the next day one of Dan's roles was to serve Hilja, her groom, and their guests the Christian rite of communion. He conducted this reenactment of the grand drama of spiritual atonement and reconciliation with a broken hand, now visibly marked by a fresh cast. The sign was unmistakable: even those who live as larger-than-life peacemakers share the brokenness common to us all. They, too, require the assurance of a healing and reconciliation beyond human devising.

4

Enfranchising Others

I

Dan's tracks cover nearly every imaginable corner of Afghanistan: the warrens of the city bazaars, the desolate highlands, the valley wheat fields and orchards, the shepherds' shelters and mountain pastures, the sixteen-thousand-foot passes of the Silk Route, and the precincts of shrines and mosques. His pursuit of friendship and mutual trust led him into the enclaves of both military commanders and their insurgent foes. His footprints even extend to the bottom of a mineshaft in Dara-i-Suf, hundreds of yards below the surface, where he went to meet with miners on their own ground. These forays were rarely, if ever, about his expertise or heroic intervention; they were about helping Afghans employ their own creativity and drive to forge a better future.

Afghanistan is a storehouse of mineral riches, though its roiling history has kept most of them secret and beyond modern reach. The blue fire locked in the gemstones the world knows as lapis lazuli comes from the Hindu Kush. The endless mountain folds hold gold, copper, rubies, iron, lithium, natural gas, oil, and coal. High-grade coal.

For decades, the people south of Mazar-i-Sharif have lowered themselves, sometimes on ropes, into the maw of mountain country to retrieve the coal that keeps them warm in winter and fuels the distant cities; trucks come from far-away urban centers to haul away what is lifted out of the shafts. Rudimentary coal mining has earned the people a living in a place where drought haunts farmers, where shepherds play hopscotch with landmines, and where the landless—with few other prospects—sign on as foot soldiers in the war.

There are the inevitable reports of injuries and loss of life in the lands south of Mazar-i-Sharif, where coal seams plunge to great depths and diggings are rarely shored up. Frequent rock falls, coal dust, and lethal gases take their toll in the absence of safety equipment or devices to monitor conditions.

Despite having no training as a mining engineer, Dan took his curiosity and native ingenuity hundreds of yards down into the darkness, where the faint voices of miners echoed up the shafts. One of the most penetrating images from Dan's years among the Afghans is the moment when his feet touched the bottom of the shaft in almost total darkness and he peered into the smudged faces of Afghan miners, who gazed back into the eyes of this foreigner in astonishment.

They sat together in faint candlelight as Dan listened to the travails of those who drag coal out of the earth's depths. As he and the miners groped their way along the coalface, assessing what might be done, together they devised a plan to spare the miners' health and better their lives.

II

A survival skill in areas of smoldering conflict is negotiating frequent and dicey roadblocks. These chokeholds along the road network give police, the army, or a variety of other armed groups pressure points that can yield handsome dividends. When salaries arrive intermittently and are laughable even when paid, roadblocks can supplement a gunman's living. The line between legitimate authority and highway robbery disappears in the choking road dust.

For travelers, whether drivers or passengers, effectively coping with roadblocks is an art form requiring a keen eye for hidden grievances that can set fire to the most innocent gesture or remark. So skilled was Dan at reading the profile of these roadblock dangers—having learned from his own early stumbles—he later schooled others in the fine art.

But Dan probed for much more at these danger points than a way past the hazards. He recognized that the glassy-eyed young men slung with weapons at these roadblocks arrived there having nowhere else to go. The realities of war—hazardous fields, vulnerable families, failed education, personal powerlessness, and boredom—drove them into the embrace of armed groups and drug addiction. Poppies, the last resort of those who can still farm, have taken a pernicious toll among Afghan young men, who curse themselves for having been born into such desperate and barren times.

As Dan traveled in the provinces, he observed that an entire generation of able-bodied men might be lost unless some intervention could halt the drift into alienation and addiction. Yet war had focused awareness, priorities, and government resources elsewhere. There would be little interest or wherewithal to meet this invisible crisis.

With a graduate degree in counseling from West Virginia University, Dan had a framework for understanding the problem at hand and possible ways to address it. His many years of community involvement in Hazara country had persuaded him of the power of small beginnings. He knew that broad solutions are often most effective when based on small-scale ventures that grow out of local initiative.

Four young opium-addicted Afghans from Laghman Province once presented themselves to Dan, asking to undergo treatment. He took them to a Kabul hospital, where they were required to go off opium. Once beyond the agonies of withdrawal, the hospital could no longer shelter them. Sending them back to the desolate circumstances that had led them into their addiction would surely result in relapse.

Shelter was at a premium in a city thronged with people displaced by the danger and harsh conditions in the provinces, so there was little chance of finding housing for four young Afghans battling serious drug dependency. In the end, given the urgent need, Dan and Seija vacated their own flat and turned it over to the young men as a halfway house where they could recover and prepare for a new life.

The wisdom Dan and Seija reaped from this chapter in the struggle for Afghanistan boils down to something like this: coming face-to-face with edgy young gunmen at a roadblock might cost you more than *baksheesh* (a gratuity); it might cost you your home.

III

One way to take the measure of a person is to note the things that tend to happen when that person is present. An Afghan woman experienced in community health, Dr. Shukria Hassan, tells a story in which Dan was not a main actor but, typical of his manner, served as a fruitful presence.

The late Dr. Carl Taylor, a world leader in public health, developed an innovative method of pregnancy and childbirth education that consists simply of gathering mothers into learning circles in which they recite the stories of their own pregnancies, deliveries, and infant care. These stories, one by one, become the syllabus for high-energy learning about women's survival and health. After being introduced to this method, Dr. Hassan took it into the Afghan field—with Dan at the Jeep's helm, forging a way into remote highland settlements where clinic assignments entail such hardship that even nurses and midwives refuse to serve there.

The isolation of some these mountain settlements often meant a whole day's walk through winter snows. Dr. Hassan and Seija, a trained midwife, describe meeting with dreadful health challenges in these settlements. Cramped living in winter shelters frequently gave rise to pneumonia, meningitis, tuberculosis, and a variety of skin infections. Maternal mortality in such conditions runs riot, as does early infant death. In the absence of healthcare workers, desperate villagers take loved ones with convulsions and other alarming symptoms to the *mullahs*[1] at the local mosques for spiritual therapy. Seija and Dan would tell of performing urgent amputations by lantern light with nothing but a Swiss army knife.

The first port of call in working with such communities is the *shura*, or elders' council. Composed entirely of older men, chief among them the local religious authority, these *shuras* were Dan's second home. He could be seen sitting with the men in patient and earnest give-and-take, seeking common ground on key issues. Soaring rhetoric peppered with proverbs, witty turns of phrase, and recitations of history and the holy writings were the order of the day even in the humblest settlements. It was Dan's role to turn these rhetorical flourishes to the advantage of better health and opportunity, especially for women and children.

The local *shuras* had misgivings about the women-only workshops that the outsiders were promoting. Designed to gather younger women and mothers for the purpose of sharing and learning about the intimate topics of childbirth and infant care, the concept ran counter to the elders' understanding of gender, age, and

---

1. *Mullah*: title given to some Islamic clergy

A *shura*, or elders' council, deliberates in a remote settlement. Such groups of community leaders were Dan's second home. Photograph by Dan Terry.

propriety. With Dan present, though, the locals and outsiders hammered out a compromise: the younger women's mothers-in-law would be permitted to participate in the learning circles. They in turn would impart their learning to their younger family members.

For the inaugural women-only workshop, the planners expected a circle of thirty participants. To their surprise, fifty elderly women, birth attendants, and others showed up seeking admission. As the participants began openly recounting for the first time what were formerly the secret events of their lives, a remarkable dynamic took hold. In the workshops the lilt of voices rose and eyes sparkled with recognition and discovery. The women recounted their stories of grief for lost infants and children and found comfort in the larger sisterhood. There followed shouts and laughter, nutritious feasting, and even dancing into the wee hours.

The positive effect of this simple but powerful learning method may be read in the plummeting maternal and infant mortality rates across Afghanistan. What began as earnest discussions in tiny settlement *shuras* and women's gatherings in the central highlands is now replicated by Afghan government mandate across the country. Young women and mothers, who have successfully barged onto the scene in impressive numbers, can no longer be excluded. They, with the *shuras*, acknowledge the substantial good that has flowed to their communities in this transforming process.

Were a mural to depict this scene of empowered Afghan women and their communities, it would prominently feature women such as Dr. Hassan who conceived, proved, and replicated dramatic and life-saving initiatives. Upon careful examination, a viewer might see at the margins of the tableau a rumpled, bearded figure with an expression of satisfaction wreathing his face.

IV

Dan's driveway often resembled a scrapyard littered with vehicles in various stages of resurrection. This was not an objectionable state of affairs in a land where motorized transport, whatever the aesthetic qualities, is highly prized. Once, a Toyota van in Dan's yard caught the eye of a coworker, Jim Couch, who wondered if it might be for sale. It could meet the transport need of a project in Faizabad, he explained. Dan seemed pleased at the prospect of assisting a worthy program and agreed to meet Jim and an associate for a test drive around the city.

As they set out through the crowded streets, Dan announced that he had a "small visa matter" to sort out. Dan and his passengers would have known very well that a "small visa matter" was an oxymoron. Nevertheless, in blinding rain, Dan parked the van at a busy corner and vanished into the bazaar for an extended time. In this city where car bombs are not unknown, a nervous policeman approached, peered warily into the van, and ordered Dan's passengers to move the vehicle immediately. With that, the test drive was derailed until Dan, the van, and the interested buyers could reassemble.

At their next attempt, Dan launched into a full-blown plan for refurbishing the vehicle. "Really, if you want to keep this van," he told them with a sweep of his hand, "you should tear out this entire dashboard and replace it with new equipment. And the transmission needs to be beefed up if you want to run it to Faizabad." By now, the prospective buyers were staring out the windows, wondering if this might be more information than they had bargained for.

But Dan was not nearly finished. "And a driver," he inquired. "Have you thought about who you might hire as a driver for the van? Since the route to Faizabad passes through contested country, you really ought to hire a Pashtun. As it happens, I know just such a person. He could safely shuttle between Faizabad and Kabul, bringing fresh produce into the bazaar."

Somehow, the sale of a thoroughly used van of doubtful dashboard and transmission had become a piece of a vast peacebuilding enterprise. What had begun as a simple commercial transaction had become a concept that could improve the nutritional status of Kabulis and address the lamentable rates of unemployment among Pashtun drivers.

The van never made it to Faizabad, and the Pashtun driver may still be looking for work, but the best of this failed transaction survives: it remains the story of truthful daily dealings, humble though they were, knotted into some larger pattern for building a lasting peace.

V

Though Dan had decided tastes in music and landscapes, in matters of food he was a zealous and unbiased omnivore. Without exception, his Afghan friends agree that he devoured with unguarded zest whatever was placed before him, including the local stew of sheep tail fat. As a youngster Dan had earned a reputation for consuming Himalayan quantities of *sooji* and *dalia*, hearty wheat porridges favored in north India. These, he said, provided honest wherewithal for a whole day's trekking.

For Dan, peanut butter slathered on yesterday's leftover *naan* was royal fare. He could rhapsodize on the nutritional and metaphysical merits of peanut butter, which, in his estimation, came close to being the staff (or spread) of life. Indeed, one of Dan's most insistent—and self-interested—development proposals was the launching of a peanut butter processing business. Though he made a blustery show of consuming it in prodigious quantities, his savvy Afghan friends saw quickly that the potential market for peanut butter locally was likely not larger than one man: Dan. His rationale that peanut butter consumption would rectify national nutritional deficits made no dent in their skepticism.

Of all the foods that came from his childhood family kitchen in India, none pleased Dan quite so much as batches of cinnamon rolls. These, married to dollops of peanut butter, came frightfully close to nirvana. When, during his parents' absences from Mussoorie, he would come to live in the Woodstock School boys' dorm he always arrived fortified with a box of these homemade rolls.

Much later, when he and Seija would travel in North America to visit family and churches, Dan discovered the over-the-top American franchise Cinnabon. Its rolls were the antithesis of hardscrabble life in the Hindu Kush and an offense to sober conscience, sound nutrition, and world justice. But Dan could not help himself. The aromas wafting down airport concourses or mall walkways took him utterly hostage.

Despite a lifetime of bushwhacking through mountain wildernesses far beyond the reach of modern amenities, by all accounts Dan was clueless when it came to cooking. His youngest daughter, Saara, recalls a time when they were muddling along at home in Afghanistan while the rest of the family was away. Dan fancied that a chicken would lift their morale, so he purchased a live fowl from the market. The travails of plucking and dressing the chicken finally accomplished, Dan proposed that they should boil the chicken for a long time to ensure tenderness. Haunted by thoughts that it might still be undercooked, he then baked it in the oven. Still not quite convinced that it was safe to consume, he lastly passed it through the frying pan.

It is called thrice-cooked chicken in the cookbook he never published.

VI

Dan's instincts for reading murky circumstances in Afghanistan so often brought him out of danger, he did not always listen to the judgments of his foreign coworkers. He had lived through too much history to begin doubting his own capacities, particularly when considering the opinions or instructions of those far less experienced than he. In this way, too, Dantri had become decidedly Afghan; he believed that his graying beard and hair should count for something.

Dan proposed one day to take a handful of his foreign colleagues on a day's excursion into the mountains outside Kabul. As they were leaving the capital they passed the stadium, where a national celebration was underway that included the president, his senior officials, and the diplomatic community. Shortly after Dan and his party left the city, gunmen in an adjoining apartment block raked the stadium stands with gunfire and rockets. Though the president escaped harm, others were wounded and some killed.

As the news of the tragedy spread, an International Assistance Mission (IAM) administrator texted Dan's group to say they should return to the city immediately for their own safety. But with trouble behind them and the prospect of a day in the hills still ahead, the party agreed that it would be safer to hike the backcountry with Dan than to return to mayhem in the city.

"Hiking with Dan" in the Himalayas was an oxymoron, however. His strides were so long and his pace so ferocious that he would quickly outdistance any companion. One fit trailmate quite used to the mountains conceded, "And I thought I was good!" Dan would soon disappear around the shoulder of the next ridge, only to reappear on a distant outcrop to shout encouragement and point out the best route. Those who knew his ways, though, would describe how, out of sight, he would circle around and above those who followed to be sure they were holding up. They would find him waiting in the shade of an overhang or on a summit, ready to offer a grand tour of local lore or identify points of interest.

None of Dan's stories or guidance was delivered with quite as much authority as his insistence on greeting and chattering with shepherds and others encountered on the way. It seemed his mantra was, "Small talk is peace." The slipstream of Dan's earnest and buoyant "*Salaams*" and irrepressible humor left surprised joy as its wake. His companions did their best to keep pace.

The day in the hills at an end, the party made its way back into Kabul, where they were met by an angry agency administrator. Why had they ignored his instruction to return to the city? How could they prefer their own whim to his explicit request? The pattern of Dan's independent judgment, long a strong suit that had carried him into Afghanistan's heart when so many others had fallen short, had now come between him and chagrined agency leaders.

VII

As profoundly as Dantri's outsized gestures, humor, and unswerving goodwill impressed the Afghans, they also

left an enduring impression on many of his Western colleagues—even those who disagreed with his approach
and those who had only passing encounters with him.

One acquaintance, who worked in development in
Asia for many years and knew Dan only briefly, said,

> He is the single most influential person upon my
> life course. We would walk the gullies of the Amu
> Darya Valley together, the Russian steppes stretch-
> ing away to the north, and it was clear from his
> musing that he had somehow succeeded in climb-
> ing right inside the culture, mind, and language of
> the Afghan people. I sometimes had the feeling,
> too, that he was looking out on these things not
> from ground level but from some great height.

Dan's influence extended far beyond his agency
peers, this colleague says, something he witnessed during weeks of service alongside the community at Lal wa
Sar Jangal to open an airstrip. The Hazaras turned out
in impressive numbers with hand implements to create this link to the outside world. With his verve and
willingness to share in the manual labor, Dan inspired
the villagers at Lal to take ownership of the project.
Another colleague, a surgeon, confesses with some
reticence, "No one knew Afghanistan better than Dan.
And Afghanistan knew Dan. With him, the six degrees
of separation were halved. It was never more than three.
And that counts for everything with mountain people."

Dan's singular web of friendship and grasp of
Afghan values, mores, and dreams led one veteran
development colleague to say,

> When the movers and shakers gathered in Bonn
> [in December 2001] to make a plan for the "new"
> Afghanistan, the experts were at hand: Pentagon
> planners, the politically savvy, and the warlords.
> But it wasn't enough. It miscarried because they
> lacked a Dan Terry. He might have helped to
> bridge the yawning divide between perception

Dan (right) and two companions wrestle with a balky 4x4. Photograph by Dan Jantzen, used with permission.

and reality. He would have anchored the whole enterprise in the truth of mountain life, steered them past the hazards that now bedevil us all.

VIII

The summer of 2001 blew an ill wind on humanitarian workers in Afghanistan. The Taliban regime had begun to question the intent of Western aid workers after discovering at a roadblock that a charity, Shelter Now International (SNI), possessed Christian religious material, including videos and printed matter. The regime considered this proselytizing, which was utterly forbidden. The workers in question and their Afghan helpers were detained, and alarm spread among Taliban leaders that other Western humanitarian workers might also be surreptitiously spreading the Christian message.

In addition to SNI, Taliban suspicion and concern fastened on another Christian charity: IAM, active since 1966, primarily in eye care and public health. Ignoring IAM's protests that they were innocent, the authorities ordered the organization to close down its work and evacuate all personnel within seventy-two hours. Dan and Seija, who at that time were still serving under IAM, needed to leave.

Communicating these dire developments to Dan and Seija's remote location, Lal wa Sar Jangal, was not a simple matter. Satellite phone contact was intermittent, and the journey west from Kabul took many hours. When IAM officials finally established a phone link with Dan and Seija, twenty-four hours had already passed. Other IAM personnel had left in haste for Peshawar, Pakistan. With the exit deadline approaching, the IAM officials' plea was stark: "Get out! *Now!*"

Dan rarely took such developments very seriously. He had been around long enough to discount the breathlessness that often accompanied such ultimatums. His clear-eyed take more often than not was, "This, too, shall pass." What is more, he was persuaded that it was possible to conduct reasonable discussion even with the Taliban when differences or difficulties arose. Indeed, when news of the exit deadline for IAM workers arrived, Dan was closeted in extended dialogue with the local *shura*, the council of elders, and expressed reluctance to leave.

But Seija understood the seriousness of the hour, and she prevailed in the decision to depart immediately. Before they left, though, Dan and Seija had to close the hospital in Lal wa Sar Jangal and entrust its care to local staff. Patients had to be dismissed and workers paid their salaries and severance. They had to pack their personal gear and say goodbye to a shocked community and bewildered friends. Beyond that, many hours of punishing country separated them from the Pakistan border.

Knowing that traveling the roads would bring them to checkpoints where they could lose precious hours or even face detention at the hands of suspicious local authorities, Dan improvised a route to the frontier that would skirt these hazards. He plunged along the dry riverbeds, poppy fields, and rarely-used mountain tracks leading eastward to the frontier. ("You never know when a side road might come in handy.")

By the time Dan and Seija arrived at the mountain frontier crossing to Pakistan, the world press and agency executives were waiting in a state of foreboding. From there they were conducted to Peshawar, where fellow workers had largely despaired of their safety, thinking they might well have disappeared into Taliban detention.[2]

The ensuing intervention of the West swiftly altered Afghanistan's political landscape and permitted IAM and its workers to return. It also initiated a new decade of unremitting bloody struggle.

---

2. A note on context: At the time, Osama bin Laden had received mention in the world press with regard to the bombings at the U.S. embassies in East Africa and failed American missile strikes on his training camps in eastern Afghanistan, but in late August 2001 bin Laden was not yet a global icon of terror. Just two weeks after Dan and Seija's hurried departure through the vicinity of Osama's operations, the world was transfixed by the September 11 attacks in America. Thereafter, hardly any corner of the planet would fail to recognize bin Laden's name.

5

Unarmed and Dangerous

I

The work of a peacemaker in Afghanistan in the first decade of the twenty-first century faced a mountainous agenda: friendships to be forged with the Taliban and other mountain recalcitrants; vexing questions of interfaith conversation to be addressed; competing interests to be reconciled; and the need to deal with the many foreign forces that had inserted themselves into Afghanistan's troubles. Conflicts of gender, generation, ethnicity, and ideology threatened ambush around nearly every corner. In one letter to friends, Dan observed, "The first rule of thumb in nearly every situation here is to acknowledge conflict." All told, Afghanistan offered a field of riches for one with a peacemaker's calling.

Dan also noticed small and seemingly insignificant personal fractures. Ever mindful of the outsider, he had a practiced and instinctive eye for those at the margins of community—and he moved towards them.

A doctor acquaintance of Dan's tells one such story, far from the dramas of life-and-death struggle. The doctor's Catholic spirituality had not always met with understanding among fellow Christian workers, who found his theology and spirituality somehow alien. "With Dan, I found a natural comfort and welcome," he remembers.

> He put me at ease in several ways. First, it was evident that Dan also found beauty and meaning in liturgy, and he took pains to reflect that to me. That this was more than polite concession became clear when he himself would sometimes lead our devotional gatherings with elements of liturgy like the Lord's Prayer. Sometimes I even glimpsed myself in his manner. I saw in these small gestures heaven's work of peacemaking within the Christian family.
>
> And then there came a day when the [Muslim] Afghan workers at the hospital asked for a place to pray. As a Christian institution, this touched off real soul-searching. Some felt that to grant the request would betray our identity. At the same time, we didn't want to fail the test of hospitality. We were a divided house. Groping for answers, I sought out Dan.

Dan's counsel upended prevailing logic, the doctor recounts. "Providing a place of prayer for your workers, far from thwarting your ministry, will prove to be an open door," Dan predicted. "It will enhance and strengthen what you have been called here to do."

With some uncertainty, says the doctor, the Christian hospital staff set aside a portion of the rose garden, planted some trees and shrubs to provide shelter from wind and weather, and installed an ablution facility for ceremonial washing.

On the day of the prayer garden's opening, the doctor joined his Muslim coworkers in answering their call to prayer, and knelt as a Christian. He sensed the goodness of the place to which events and providential leading had brought them. An advisor to President

Hamid Karzai, who was present on the hospital grounds that day, observed, "This is what we have been seeking. This is the peace we dream of."

In the following months, Dan's prophetic word about the ministry of the hospital proved its full worth. "How much richer we now find ourselves," the doctor says. "Richer in faith and calling. Richer in friendship with our Afghan coworkers."

On a hospital grounds in Kabul, there remains a corner of a rose garden redolent of prayer and a possible, waiting peace.

II

Dan was nothing if not a spiritually rooted and persuaded Christian, but that proved no hindrance to finding his place in a deeply traditional Muslim society. Indeed, he would say, it offered him a spiritual highway. Dan was often a guest in mosques that doubled as lodges for travelers in remote settings. There he was seen, barefoot and cross-legged on the carpets, taking tea in earnest conversation with the local religious leaders, the *imams*, and the community *shuras*. His mastery of the nuances of manner and language in these religious settings, together with his courtly respect, wakefulness to what was stirring beneath the surface, and thoughtful insights intrigued his hosts wherever he wandered.

On one occasion in a particularly poor mosque in Gardez, where the faithful lacked even a carpet and gathered to kneel in prayer on a covering of wheat chaff, the *imam* refused to believe that Dantri could be anything but a Muslim. Judging from Dan's demeanor, he heartily maintained that Dan *had to be* a Muslim. Persuaded finally, but believing that he must not be far from status as a faithful, the *imam* enjoined Dan, "I will give you a wife, a sheep, and a house if you declare yourself a Muslim."

Dan replied, "God, in mercy, has already granted me a wife, a sheep, and a home. What is still lacking is a place to foster the health of your village neighbors. Build a clinic here, and I will be perfectly content."

Dan's reputation for such grace and absence of any judgment lingered long. One Afghan coworker (with a touch of hyperbole, no doubt) voiced an oft-repeated assertion about Dan. "I tell you," he averred solemnly, "Dantri was more Afghan than we Afghans, and he was more Muslim than we Muslims." As for the qualities that define that "Afghan-ness"—trustworthiness, loyalty, and sacred hospitality—Dantri passed the test as a fully paid-up member of the community.

But what, then, of his "Muslim-ness"? How could he, a Christian infidel who had never been on *hadj*[1] or bound himself to the daily prayers, fasts, and other duties of the Muslim faithful—have been thought of as conforming to the best of Islam? A fair question, his Muslim friends say. In the greatest commandments of our scriptures, they explain—to practice humility; to be generous to widows, the orphans, and the poor; and to be selfless and persevering in the search for justice and peace—Dantri was more Muslim than we Muslims.

Just as striking—given Dan's comfort at a religious interface often acrid with fear, suspicion, loathing, and bloodletting—is that many in the Christian community also revered him. This is particularly true of the children of his coworkers, who idolized Dan's nonconformity, moral courage, and flair for the improbable. Those children made known, sometimes to their parents' chagrin, their ambition to one day be like him.

When Dan and Seija felt the need for a break from the turbulence of life in the Hindu Kush, they found respite in the Indian hill town of Mussoorie, where he had lived as a boy and where their own children

---

1. *Hadj*: pilgrimage to Mecca, Saudi Arabia, that Muslims are required to make

studied at Woodstock School. When in Mussoorie, they would worship in a gray stone church set in a mountain saddle above the school campus and surrounded by colonial-era buildings in stands of oak and cedar. To the northeast, on a clear day one can see from there the ermine summits of Nanda Devi and Bandar Poonch, landmarks of the high Himalayas.

One Sunday morning, witnesses say, as the faithful met for worship, Dan and Seija arrived just as the preacher was exhorting the community to pray for the peoples of the world. Acquainted with the Terrys and their service, the preacher broke away from his prepared message and summoned Dan, attired in full Afghan regalia, to join him. Dan moved to the front, his arms raised in a devotional gesture reminiscent of prayer in the mosques, and took his place next to the minister. The minister asked him, "So tell us, Dan, how should we pray for the Afghans?"

A brief silence followed. Then Dan replied, "What I can tell you is this. It must be with great love. Above all, we must love them."

III

However rich Dan found his experience in Afghanistan, one cost of the isolation was scant opportunity to worship with other Christians. Though Dan was hardly conventional in expressing his faith, he and Seija looked forward to occasions when they could share openly with fellow Christians in familiar ways.

When they left Afghanistan in haste in late August 2001, it became clear how deeply he was affected by the well-worn traditions of the Christian faith. Despite relief in finding personal safety, Dan and Seija and their coworkers had to face several stark truths: the harrowing journey they had just completed, the heartbreak of goodbyes to friends in Afghanistan, the sting of expulsion by the Taliban government, and the prospect that they might not be permitted to return to a land and to work for which they cared deeply. Burdened by the weight of these thoughts, Dan and his colleagues gathered for prayer, worship, and reflection. A gospel song of personal testimony and assurance opened the occasion:

> Amazing grace, how sweet the sound that saved a
> wretch like me!
> I once was lost, but now am found, was blind,
> but now I see.
> Through many dangers, toils and snares, I have
> already come.
> 'Tis grace hath brought me safe thus far, and grace
> will lead me home.

As the voices filled the room, the lyrics rang with rare meaning. Dan was so overcome with gratitude and deep emotion that he sank weakly to the floor, clinging to Seija for support. The exquisite gift of community in faith, the recognition of mercy in precarious circumstances, the experience of blessing despite failures and flaws: these had their full effect on Dan.

In the days that followed, having found again his root of inner strength, Dan became a voice for courage and hope among his colleagues. No one should despair, he told them. All was not lost. A further chapter in the story would yet be written.

IV

It would be fair to ask whether the romance between Dan and his Finnish wife, Seija—begun in the wild recesses of Hazara country and pursued through the twists and thorny turns of thirty years in the Hindu Kush—could survive. No love, however deep, can escape completely the battering of long absences amid uncertainty and bloodletting. The fact that Dan and Seija raised three daughters in addition to tending each other in such slippery circumstances is little short of extraordinary; there were ample occasions along the way for a couple's bonds to bruise and fray.

An Afghan family friend provides a glimpse of a moment in Kabul that may hold a key to Dan and Seija's perseverance.

> One day, Dantri asked me to go into the bazaar to find a horse cart for the evening, one of the *wallahs*[2] who transport potatoes and produce around the city. This I could not understand, because Dantri had his own Afghan Jeep for transport. So why should he want a horse cart to take him around? But I did as he asked and brought a horse cart and its driver to the front gate. Then I told him, "Dantri, the cart you wanted is here." He came out to examine the cart and seemed pleased that the horse was also decorated with colored cloth and sequins. Then he disappeared into the house, and I could hear him calling Seija, his wife. When they returned, Dantri bent over, quite surprising her by picking her up in his arms and seating her in the cart. Then he climbed in next to her. He gave instructions to the driver, and then turning, said to his wife, "Seija, tonight is the anniversary of our wedding, and I am taking you to the Intercontinental Hotel for dinner." They rode away into the streets to the great amusement of neighbors and bazaar-goers.

V

Dan's vocation as peacemaker frequently followed him into his friendships. A friend in the Appalachian Mountains recalls a time after she had separated from her husband. Dan had only just returned to North

---

2. *Wallah:* a vendor or person associated with a particular duty

Dan and Seija Terry. Photograph used with permission of CURE International.

America and was still exhausted from the exertions of
life in the Hindu Kush when he learned this unhappy
news. But he drove out on the county roads to find her.
They sat side by side on the porch of her mountain
cottage, looking out over the summer hills.

> It was as though he needed to see through my eyes
> that day," she says. "He came to see me to offer
> comfort, for sure, but equally much to understand
> . . . This is the deep work of friendship. It reflects
> Dan's commitment to bridging the gaps, his abil-
> ity to hold multiple views of a human situation,
> his enjoyment of different personalities. . . . It was
> a moment of healing for me. That one who braved
> the battle lines in Central Asia appealing for peace
> should come to find me in my private grief: this
> was a rare gift, to find peace in the presence of an
> unexpected friend.

Dan's calling as peacemaker touched his family,
too. Though the family's work had scattered them to
far-flung reaches of the globe and long years of absence

divided members from each other, Dan's younger sister Ruth remembers a particularly healing conversation. Unsettled by issues of identity that sometimes haunt children born and raised far from their parents' origins, she found herself at bitter odds with the excesses and flaws of the North American world. In a quiet moment with his sister, Dan observed, "But when we live in India or Afghanistan, we are happy to withhold our judgment of those cultures whose manifold imperfections we know well. Might we not be just as forgiving of the faults we find here?"

That question, says Ruth, set her on a path beyond anger and confusion. The salve of grace, like a peacemaker's vocation, applies whatever the time and place.

VI

Although the business of peacemaking is weighty, stressful, and often risky, some of the world's most accomplished peacemakers—the likes of Desmond Tutu, Nelson Mandela, Mother Teresa, and the Dalai Lama—possess an impish humor and an itch to play. It may well be that play moves the world.

Because his own early fantasies had featured him in the cockpit of some plane, riding some sturdy bike, or driving an all-terrain vehicle, Dan could read such dreams in the faces of children. He was quick to secretly abet those unspoken—and slightly illicit—fancies. A perfect occasion for such tomfoolery presented itself when Dan led a convoy of vehicles beyond city confines for a daylong excursion. A favorite destination was Tanghi, a canyon not far from Mazar-i-Sharif, near the spot where the local commander who later became a trusted friend had once held Dan hostage.

The Terry Jeep usually carried more children than the other vehicles did—or than the law would normally approve—for the simple reason that Dan would allow the youngsters to slip into the driver's seat, by turn, on deserted stretches of road. Perched in Dan's lap, the younger ones would thrill at hanging onto the steering wheel, while the older ones driving on their own also mastered the heart-pounding manipulation of clutch, gears, and accelerator. All the while Dan would offer a stream of counsel on how to negotiate rugged country, avoid the ruts, and change a flat tire. On their way home Dan sometimes took the convoy of adults and children via the base of the once-feared commander and his swaggering gunmen, who seemed happy to share a cup of *chai* with the canyon visitors.

Dan's youngest daughter, Saara, remembers traveling once with her father from Kabul to Lal wa Sar Jangal, their former home in Hazara country. Although Saara was only fourteen years old at the time, Dan had given her the wheel of the Jeep. Before long she and Dan passed some travelers on foot. Dan directed Saara to pull over so he could offer them a ride. They thronged the vehicle, filling the available spaces with their assorted bundles. Having settled themselves, the riders took stock of the situation and were shocked to realize that a teenager was behind the wheel. And a blonde girl at that!

It was an early sign that, even in mountain backcountry, play just might be changing the world.

VII

After nearly a decade of war pitting the Taliban and their allies against the American-led coalition, the International Security Assistance Force (ISAF) had spread fear and uncertainty to many quarters of eastern and southern Afghanistan. Whether by summary executions, night raids, bombings, or hostage-taking, people in the cities and open country dreaded becoming collateral damage—or worse, targets. Stringent safety measures were *de rigueur* everywhere.

Foreigners entering the country, whatever their work, were expected to have contingency plans for personal safety. One American humanitarian worker recounts that, having arrived in Kabul, he attended a mandatory orientation session with an embassy security officer. The officer wanted to know what protective arrangements he had put in place. The worker replied that he felt reasonably safe and saw no need for special measures. Scoffing at such naïveté, the embassy officer mocked the cluelessness of the new arrival.

The worker thought for a moment and then replied, "Well, I do have something of a security plan. If I'm ever in trouble, I'll give Dan Terry a call." By this time, Dan had earned a reputation as a good-faith go-between among warring factions.

A long silence followed the worker's comment. Then the embassy official conceded, "Actually, I couldn't think of a better plan myself."

VIII

In a land awash with arms and munitions, where guns are an article of everyday clothing for many, Dan never packed heat. But he engaged with attentive compassion the many who did carry guns—whether the Taliban or those of the opposing coalition forces, including Alliance warlords and members of the Karzai government.

In such a context, it is intriguing to stumble upon the traditional Afghan saying, "An unarmed Pashtun is more dangerous than an armed one." While there is ambiguity in all such proverbs, this apparent Afghan appreciation of a power greater than the gun is fascinating. This force of defenselessness, which endangers the ruling logic of war and violence, was the power upon which Dan drew for his work and life. One of Dan's companions recalls the following incident.

> Dan and I were once crossing the poppy fields of Bamian in the Beast [another name for the renowned "Afghan Jeep"]. We stopped around

midday in the shade of roadside trees for lunch. From behind nearby cover there emerged a young boy, not more than fourteen years old, who trained a rifle on us as he approached. Taut with fear, the boy was playing no game. I reached slowly for a concealed weapon. But Dan whispered restraint as he stepped out of the Jeep, his arms outstretched in a characteristic gesture of prayer and embrace, showing that he posed no threat. "Son, we mean you no harm," he said in measured, fatherly voice. With no apparent fear of the rifle's muzzle, Dan walked directly into the line of fire—in part, I am sure, to keep me from taking the kid out. Finally, he enfolded the young boy gently in his great wingspan. . . . The boy began to shake with sobs and tears for having found safety in the embrace of a total stranger he had taken for an enemy.

Back in the shelter of the Jeep, an armed adult sweaty with fear witnessed the strange truth of that Afghan proverb. An unarmed person can be more "dangerous" than an armed one.

6

Delicate Transactions

I

Dan discovered early on that seeking peace between warring sides is mostly an inglorious, behind-the-scenes, messy business, and no one emerges from the fray with unsoiled hands or ideals. Even the stories can hardly be divulged, given the need to protect those involved, who could become targets if identified. This is never truer than when imminent threat places ordinary communities in the crosshairs.

It so happened that an American drone went down in a wilderness region of Afghanistan and fell into the hands of a Taliban commander who recognized its potential value. The American-led coalition forces prepared overwhelming force to retrieve or destroy the drone's operating system, which they could not permit to fall into unfriendly hands. If allowed to run their lethal course, the actions would bring hellfire down not only on the commander and his gunmen but also on any man, woman, or child unlucky enough to live in the vicinity.

Dan recognized that, however sullied the intentions and practices of the opposing sides, everything must be done to protect the innocents who would otherwise suffer in the impending clash. Employing a personal channel of contact with the insurgent commander in question, he helped to facilitate an agreement that would return the hardware to the American military and spare the community further insult, injury, and death.

Having failed once, the delicate transaction was rescheduled to take place in a tunnel, which would protect the wary insurgents from aerial attack or ambush. At the appointed hour a ramshackle pickup, bearing the drone's wreckage, came winding out of the mountain wilderness. A flatbed truck, meanwhile, approached from the opposite direction. In that darkened passage, they drew up alongside each other and made the transfer. The two vehicles and parties then backed away from each other, avoiding any further bloodshed and preserving the lives of the innocents most at risk.

When historians write their accounts of the war and what happened on those embattled mountain slopes, they will likely not record the events of that day when Afghan villagers were spared the fury of modern military power. But the children and their parents in that community may well remember the name *Dantri*, the one who loved even a tainted scrap of peace.

II

When American student of theology Gary Moorehead set out for Afghanistan in 2003, he could not have imagined the wild ride waiting for him in the Hindu Kush, with its chaotic crossing of cultures, firepower, geopolitics, humanitarian frenzy, and poverty. Once immersed in that jostling, desperate scene, he found he could not return to studying Karl Barth's dogmatics or parsing Greek verbs. What began for Gary as a visit of conscience and curiosity became a calling to volunteer aid work.

There were, of course, opportunists in Afghanistan who seized upon the promise of quick money no matter the moral or existential risks; witness the horde of profiteers, local and foreign, who made no altruistic pretense about their purposes. More complicated were the humanitarians—some neophytes, but many crusty veterans—who were thoroughly professional about setting up their operations and generating revenue with slick public appeals and the ability to secure their own grants and contracts. Also present were the professional nation-builders and technocrats: experts from every corner of the globe whose extensive resumes assured them the keys to the design of Afghanistan's future systems of education, health, commerce, governance, and even culture. Last of all were the enclave diplomats, who applied their polished skills to the favorable rearrangement of power—even as the military instruments that backed up their work massed in bases across Central Asia.

Gary Moorehead took his place as an aid worker in that scheme, learning its mores and conventions: *Be safe. Stay close. Avoid becoming a hostage or casualty. Travel seldom and only with others. Keep the walls intact, lock the gates, and activate the alarm. Guards will patrol the perimeter. Associate with locals at a minimum. Better safe than sorry.* For Gary, even the quarter-mile daylight walk to his office felt risky.

But Gary's humanitarian impulses, along with his theological training and conscience, began to rub raw under these constraints. Could the ambitious enterprise to remake Afghanistan really succeed on a cloistered, one-way street where Afghans were mostly passive spectators? Could the power brokers, diplomats, foot soldiers, and experts with armor and dollars do without ordinary Afghans as they fashioned the nation's future? He had to wonder.

Then, as winter took hold one year, Dan and Seija and their friends Tom and Libby Little invited Gary to spend Christmas with their families. As supper was being prepared, Dan ventured, "Hey, Gary, let's go for a bike ride." This was a wholly daring departure from what Gary had come to regard as prudent behavior in a city full of menace. But before Gary could raise a reasonable question, his host was wheeling his fabled bike, Precious, out the door, and motioning for Gary to use another.

Off they plunged into the streets and alleys of Kabul, bobbing and weaving, swerving among the carts, porters, trucks, motorcycles, and vendors. Dan led the way as Gary fought to follow. Up and down a ridge and across bridges they sailed, Dan keeping up a stream of effortless chatter with neighbors in the streets and doorways. After two hours, Dan finally led them onto main thoroughfares in the middle of rush hour and back to Christmas dinner.

"It would have been madness anywhere," Gary remembers. "But in Kabul? For me, it was pure exhilaration. Beautiful! Beyond therapeutic! A crazy breakout moment. And that was my introduction to Dan Terry." This wild ride past all the conventions of the international Afghanistan enterprise "ruined" Gary forever. Life on a free-flowing, two-way street had assailed all the established rules for foreigners, and he knew he could not return to the old script.

Today, Gary works in partnership with a community in northeastern Afghanistan, attentive to local vision for the modest things that make life better, including trained midwives, a school for the handicapped, and promise for the young. All in all, they are concerns remarkably similar to those that would have claimed the attention of a certain mad cyclist in Kabul.

III

A whole book could be written of Dan's escapes when he recognized what he called "the hairy eyeball"—moments when he observed the narrowing of a conversation partner's eyes, sometimes the merest flicker on the face, and got a whiff of danger.

With whispered prayers of gratitude, Dan's Afghan friends tell of harrowing moments when they insisted to Dan that it was time to leave immediately, before a flashpoint, and while darkness might still provide some cover for retreat.

Such was a visit to the vicinity of Serobi, east of Kabul, where palisaded cliffs mark the approaches to Khyber country. Dan and a companion had gone there to meet with elders at a Pashtun café. While they waited for the elders to arrive, Dan and his friend wolfed down kebabs seasoned with what Dan called "metal powder," a condiment that greatly enhances flavor but is widely suspected of causing cancer. (Moment-to-moment knife-edge living rarely offers the luxury of weighing long-term hazards. Especially when it involves grilled lamb.)

When the parties arrived, they were led into a back room that, though carpeted, was overlaid by a sobering sheet of plastic. Recounting the story now, Dan's companion whistles in disbelief, "Sheesh! Shades of *The Sopranos*!" Stilted greetings eased only slightly as the Pashtun elders satisfied themselves that no deception was at work. Tea was brought in, and sweetmeats and conversation followed. Dan's friend recalls what happened next:

> When we rose to leave at evening, the Pashtuns told us it would be foolhardy to drive home to Kabul through Serobi town, known for its lawless nights. So Dan proposed we should take a detour through the Ladeban Pass. But that route also has its issues. First, there was the snow and slush. Second, it was a favored route of bandits and gunmen. As we approached the pass, a Nissan pickup with three men drew past us and stopped up ahead. We could see the brake lights through

the falling snow. This Dan recognized as an early
hint of trouble. He eased past the truck and had
his worst suspicions confirmed: the hairy eyeball.

Dan sped away, with the Nissan now tailing
us closely. We slalomed through the snow, with
mud and slush dashing up against the windshield.
At Dan's urging, I hung out the Jeep, using my
keffiyeh[1] as a rag on the windshield so he could
make out the mountain track. From out of the
darkness there appeared furious Afghan sheepdogs that joined the melee, pelting alongside us
like dolphins chasing some darkened ship.

Mile after mile, with Dan sliding and swerving and spinning the wheel, the pickup doggedly
stayed on our tail. Never have I seen such desperate driving. It was a race for life. Our pursuers
only broke off the chase as we approached the
lights on the outskirts of Kabul. At a police check,
they veered away into the night.

Nimble feet and a sense for the "hairy eyeball" can
sometimes bring a peacemaker safely home.

IV

Afghans in Laghman Province have raw memories of the
atrocities committed by powerful invaders; the ledgers
of history are carefully tended here in the province's
valleys and forested hills. Some Laghmanis trace their
descent from the Macedonians, who marched through
in the company of Alexander the Great more than two
millennia ago. More recently, the brutalities of the Soviet
army's attempts to pacify Laghman's tribes are particularly fresh. "Razed earth" is no exaggeration in describ-
ing that bitter era when the firepower of the Red Army
came to bear on the stubborn resistance of Laghmanis.

Since it sits astride the main route from Pakistan
through the Khyber Pass to Kabul, and given its lush

---

1. *Keffiyeh*: traditional Arab cotton scarf

valleys that have long produced cucumbers, fruit, and grain for the capital's bazaars, Laghman Province could not be ignored. No wonder that it has also produced a crop of resistance fighters driven by remembered cruelties.

Chief among these fighters in recent times was Abdullah Pashtun. Michael Semple, the Irish expert on Afghanistan and friend of Dan, describes Pashtun as a "charismatic outlaw figure." "He [Pashtun] felt insulted by some badly handled ISAF security operations [in 2004] and disappeared into the mountains to raise the flag of revolt," Semple says. The area is classic outlaw country—forests of holly on the foothills, which rise away to the snow-clad peaks of Nuristan and Badakhshan.

A new round of night raids and bombing runs by the coalition forces sent a stream of disaffected and unemployed youths into the hills, where they rallied to Pashtun's cause and opened channels for smuggling timber and gemstones into Pakistan. They found willing allies in Pakistan's tribal belt, who lent them inspiration and guidance, including instruction in the production of improvised bombs. Semple summarizes, "One insulted shepherd . . . had potential to plunge the area into a cycle of violence."

While visiting northern Laghman Province, Dan and Michael heard the stories of these young men, who had sat under shade trees while being schooled by Pakistani jihadists in the technology and placement of explosive devices. This background resentment came to fever pitch one day in 2005, when Pashtun's fighters came into the sights of an American AC-130 gunship. Pinned down by deadly fire, fifteen of the Afghan fighters died on the spot. American helicopters soon whisked away the wounded and stragglers, some to detention in secret prisons. While this engagement went down in American military reports as a "clean sweep"—a resounding tactical success—its longer-range effect was to make mutual understanding an ever more remote dream. The community was left with its smoldering fury.

It was this curdled scene to which Dan and Michael Semple addressed themselves in early 2006, to see what yet might be done to ease the community's wounds. Their first step was to listen and understand. Dan and Michael drank tea with the elders' *shura* and later with aggrieved family members. As a gesture of compassion, they offered assistance to bereaved families in the form of modest compensation. The warm response this elicited included, astonishingly, embraces from Abdullah Pashtun's own father. Pashtun himself, who had survived the bloody incident, remained at arm's length somewhere in the mountains.

A short time later, at the valley's invitation, Dan returned with a health team to address the neglected condition of local families. Young men from the valley received them warmly, providing a protective escort and welcoming team members into their homes. Local Taliban authorities endorsed the trip at every turn.

That promising opening was decisively slammed shut, though, when another American airstrike killed Abdullah Pashtun and solidified his young fighters' resolve to return to the path of armed resistance. The under-the-radar work by Dan and Michael was leveled by the firepower of an armed coalition oblivious to the necessity of finding paths toward peace.

Before the airstrike, Dan and those in his company had traveled in safety on ostensibly hostile ground and were exuberantly received by the Taliban and their fighters. This is remarkable, given Dan's identity not only as a foreigner but also as an American and an infidel. It is a testament to the capacity of even those caricatured as implacable enemies to recognize goodwill from whatever the source, however modest, and to respond in kind. As one seasoned observer of the Afghan scene, Dr. Lisa Schirch, has said, "The peace that Afghanistan needs will not be delivered by helicopter."

V

After his long-standing ties with IAM were formally severed, Dan's instincts for collaboration led him into new partnerships. Future Generations, a U.S.-based aid group with whom he enjoyed bonds of friendship and common interests, formed part of this new network. Those in the wider circle of humanitarian endeavor who recognized Dan's grasp of the sweep of Afghan experience and feel for community realities sought out his gifts as well. These included agency leaders at CURE, a network of faith-based hospitals, and Michael Semple, an Irish journalist-turned-diplomat and student of the history of reconciliation in Afghanistan with whom Dan had worked in Laghman.

Dan's earlier experiences in Laghman led him into conversation with *shuras* in the province's eastern valleys, an area also reputed to be a *yaghistan*, or bandit badlands. For a time this region near the tribal belt of Pakistan had even declared itself an independent republic with its own prime minister and cabinet. Long isolated from the currents transforming other corners of Afghanistan, the Mayl and Gonapal valleys of Laghman had turned into a simmering backwater known for its poppy fields and fruitful insurgency recruiting.

But in 2006, a handful of farsighted elders, alarmed at seeing their communities marred by opium addiction and a rising tide of insurgent violence, startled many by declaring their region a "zone of peace." The elders sought to underpin that aspiration with concrete steps toward increased opportunity for young people and addressing the most compelling health needs, especially of women and families. These local impulses found their first visible expression in the construction of Tilli Primary School, a community effort that served four hundred eager boys and girls. When insurgents tried to roll back the school initiative, they were met by a resolute community—which, it must be said, was backed up by other armed groups.

Impressed with such determination, the province's education department sent one hundred sets of textbooks (each textbook to be shared by four students), which was the most help it could muster from its skimpy financial cupboard.

Dan and his colleagues were taking notice of this community moxie, and they set out to learn more about what lay behind it. A series of meetings with area councils of elders and commanders ensued as friendship and mutual confidence took hold. In time, over countless cups of tea, understanding and a partnership emerged.

That process and the plan it yielded exemplify both the hopes and gifts of the people of eastern Laghman and Dan's own accumulated wisdom and vision, method and posture. Where outside experts would usually expect local deficiencies, failure, and ignorance, Dan approached with curiosity and respect. In his view these were ancient social and natural systems that had been constructed and fine-tuned over generations. As such, they possessed proven insights and hard-won secrets deserving a measure of deference. In a letter to friends in North America, Dan explained his radically positive approach to such isolated communities. "Traditional lifestyle patterns of very low consumption of renewable resources are worth all of us studying in earnest," he wrote. "Afghanistan may be so far behind that it's way ahead."

In Dan's development work, respect for and a desire to learn from local wisdom implied a "long engagement" before any marriage, so to speak, could be contracted. It meant unhurried tea drinking in scattered venues. It meant oblique conversation with the recitation of poetry and proverbs. It required powers of listening and observation of a rare order. It required unstructured time. The success of this meandering period of betrothal would depend upon the capacity to hold one's personal interests and convictions in reserve.

Dan laid out his view of his own role in this relationship in an October 2009 letter to North American friends. "How do we mediate, mentor, [become] leaven and salt?" he asked. "Not to win hearts and minds of others to better control them. Rather to effectively squander our own hearts enfranchising and investing in them." This radical approach, Dan suggested, must be the basis of any development partnership aimed at peace in the Mayl and Gonapal valleys or beyond.

Implicit in Dan's words is a critique that leaves military campaigns—such as those "for hearts and minds" in Vietnam, Iraq, and now in Afghanistan—embarrassingly naked and ultimately subject to failure. As part of the counterinsurgency campaign, international military forces in Afghanistan have erected schools and clinics and built roads and water systems—initiatives designed to win the allegiance of local people and uncover information helpful for gaining tactical advantage. However laudable on the surface, their unintended effect is to cast suspicion on the motives of all others who do humanitarian work. The history of these alluring but suspect paths of development—on-the-quick or on-the-cheap—are the subject of knowing laughter throughout these valleys.

The Laghman plan, forged by the community itself with the help of Dan and his colleagues, is of a different variety. It states that the effort begins with "the community's initiative to identify its own interests and consensus, begin its own engagement" with outside entities, and "begin its own process of . . . reconstruction." The full inclusion of all interest groups, via "participatory decision making," the Laghman plan suggests, must drive planning and execution.

What is noteworthy about these building blocks of development is that they are not the ravings of fresh-faced idealists but rather the considered conclusions of two parties: a tested, well-worn development elder and an Afghan community on the sobering brink of ruin.

When the last of Laghman's shepherds, insurgents, and veiled women had been heard, what was it that they agreed on as matters of first importance? First, the curse of opium addiction, sometimes afflicting entire families, had to be broken. Second, the means of a dignified living had to be recreated: the mining of gemstones, the sustainable use of the forests, the husbanding of precious water for farming, and the recovery of sheepherding. Third, the health of mothers and infants had to be defended. Fourth, wintertime idleness should be turned to advantage with peer-teaching for literacy. Taken together, this was the syllabus of peace for what some have dismissed as "bandit country." It was also the fruit of a peacemaker's lifetime of searching, garnered insight, and wisdom.

Dan's drive toward partnership with the people of Laghman Province made him known in the neighboring communities of Nuristan—where he would later travel in the company of another health team, one that came to a very different end.

7

Pathos in the Backcountry

I

The Sharron Valley is as majestic, harsh, and remote as any in Afghanistan. In the summer, snowmelt feeds a silver ribbon of river, and the valley floor is strewn with stones and boulders. On each side, mountain walls rise steeply away to the crests of the Hindu Kush. As far as the eye can see, there is hardly any sign of human settlement. Not by chance is it home to the elusive snow leopard, ibex, and Marco Polo sheep.

On the silent valley floor, on a summer day in 2010, sits a caravan of three white Land Rovers. Closer examination suggests a desperate story. On small grassy mounds around the vehicles, bodies lie prostrate under a cobalt sky. Others are strewn in and under the vehicles where the victims took cover. All of them taken out execution-style. Ten in all.

The sketchiest outline of what happened there along the river emerges from the testimony of a passing shepherd who witnessed the events from the surrounding hills, and from the sole survivor, a young Afghan driver.

The story begins in the long-standing work of Tom Little, a New York optometrist whose ambition was to eliminate preventable blindness among Afghans by 2020. In addition to overseeing an eye hospital in Kabul, Tom traveled through the hinterland to serve those who could never make it to the capital city to seek treatment. In these traveling eye-care camps, Tom often sought the collaboration of others, including Dan, whose grasp of local conditions and ability to relate to Afghan communities proved useful, especially in unsettled times. They had last trekked isolated Nuristan together in 2005.

As plans took shape for a return visit to the Parun Valley in early 2010, it became clear that adding several others who could offer dental services and treat general health concerns would strengthen the team's outreach. Provision was made for interpreters, a videographer, and other support personnel. The party swelled considerably and ultimately included not only Dan and Tom but also Mahram Ali; Cheryl Beckett; Daniela Beyer; Brian Carderelli; Thomas L. Grams; Ahmed Jawed; Glen D. Lapp; Karen Woo; a young Afghan driver, Safiullah; and an Afghan health officer. Each person on the team offered useful skills, and all seemed eager for the rigors of the itinerary and the challenges it would bring.

The team held several meetings to test their commitment to the venture and to be properly oriented. In view of the physical demands of such a traverse, they ventured out on several daylong outings to gauge their capacity to stand up to rugged terrain. Dan himself had only just returned from knee surgery in North America, and he was uncertain of his own strength. The itinerary through the valley would be by foot and horseback, although Dan smuggled his mountain bike, Precious, into the cargo. During their trek, they would have twice-daily outside contact by satellite phone.

Any such endeavor would have to reckon with security risks. The area had been recently abandoned by forward-operating units of the coalition forces. But both Dan and Tom had established nationwide reputations as humanitarian workers, even among various groups of Afghan insurgents. They and the team reviewed the patterns of recent news from the region and concluded that, while nothing was risk-free, there was sound reason to believe the plan could proceed. They did, however, decide that it was prudent not to attempt the direct road approach from Kabul via Jalalabad, which would have entailed crossing uncertain country. So the team agreed to enter Nuristan ("land of light") by a safer route from the north.

Before they left, Dan and Tom obtained clearances from the relevant government authorities. They also consulted with the shadow Taliban network, which gave their assurance of safe passage. Having heard of Dan's community involvements in nearby Laghman Province, the Nuristani Taliban offered their blessing to the team's work.

And so the heart-pounding journey began. The team flew by chartered plane to the northern town of Faizabad, in Badakhshan Province, where they met the three-vehicle caravan of Land Rovers. The road approach through rugged terrain took three days, with the team spending one night in a mosque and the rest in tents in open country. They crossed the Sharron River with the vehicles and reached the road head at Naw, where they had made arrangements for eight pack-horses. A camera team documenting the travels turned back at this point.

For two days the remaining team members climbed toward a sixteen-thousand-foot pass through the mountains. Their approach was encumbered with heavy snow, preventing the horses from making progress with their loads, and the team had to abandon some of the gear on the way. They crested the pass and descended into the Parun Valley, where they stayed a night with friends. The team then trekked for eight days, conducting clinics and meeting with communities along the way. They saw and treated four hundred patients, mostly families of shepherds and subsistence farmers.

Brief video footage recovered from Dan's camera shows one scene from the trip. In a settlement of stone dwellings, several Afghan men have joined Dan in a game of rock heaving, a hilarious mountain version of shot put. It is raining, and the men are laughing as rocks soar through the air. Dan is filming the game, so although he is not visible, his voice is occasionally heard. But his enjoyment of the moment is clear in the wobble of the camera, the good-natured teasing, the way he pans from the pleased young Afghans to the mud where their rocks have come to rest. In this last glimpse of the world through Dan's eyes, he is at play with the farmers and shepherds of what is to the rest of the world a lost valley.

II

As the journey drew to a close, the medical team bid farewell to their local police escort and crossed out of Nuristan. Local villagers warned them that what had formerly been a quiet backwater in the neighboring province of Badakhshan was increasingly used by insurgents as a corridor to and from the Pakistan frontier. Undeterred and glad to be safely approaching the end of their travels, the medical team members loaded their vehicles and set out northward. On their way, they stopped to pick up three local men traveling on foot in the same direction, who appeared to know the route and promised to help them cross the approaching river.

The Sharron River, swollen by recent rains, posed a serious hazard. Experienced at fording seasonal streams, several team members waded out into the water, probing the depths with their walking sticks to find a favorable crossing. Having established the safest ford, the drivers of the three Land Rovers passed through the rocky current and drew up on the far bank, where the team stopped to share a celebratory lunch. Meanwhile, the hitchhikers they had picked up went on their way by foot, crossing the river on a downstream footbridge and disappearing from view.

As the team finished their picnic and prepared to load up their vehicles, ten gunmen rushed toward them from behind nearby boulders, firing their AK-47s and shouting "Satellite! Satellite!"—a demand for the team's satellite phones. They ordered the team members onto the ground, refusing their attempts to communicate. The gunmen swiftly executed those team members outside the vehicles and killed the two women still inside one of the Land Rovers with a grenade.

One of the team's drivers fell to his knees begging for mercy and reciting verses of the Qur'an as proof of his Muslim faith. The gunmen spared his life. Having looted some of the valuables, the killers forced the driver to carry the belongings of his murdered friends. They holed up, waiting for nightfall, and then fled on foot through the forest and into the surrounding hills. On the way, the driver reports, the gunmen communicated by radio with a commander, reporting the success of their mission. "It is all finished," they said. "We killed them."

The assassins and their terrified prisoner trekked through the night in the rugged country, the driver utterly mortified at having witnessed the death of his friends and fearing what awaited him when his usefulness came to an end. As dawn broke, his captors assured him that they intended him no harm and, to his great amazement, allowed him to walk away. When nearby villagers found the traumatized driver, the enormity of what had happened began to register. Earlier, other villagers had also raised an alarm after hearing that something untoward had happened at the river crossing.

In the meantime, dread deepened among the families and colleagues of the team members at the

protracted silence of their loved ones, who had failed
to make the expected calls from their satellite phones.
Reports of multiple deaths in a remote location were
filtering out of the area, but they were sketchy, and the
number and identities of the victims were uncertain.

The following day a unit of Badakhshan provincial
police arrived at the site of the massacre. A member
of the official party panned the riverside scene with a
camera phone as others investigated the aftermath. The
first descriptions of the terrible turn of events began to
trickle out to stunned loved ones. By the next day, a
helicopter arrived to retrieve the bodies and bring them
to Kabul.

One by one, the identities of the dead were confirmed. Phones began to ring around Afghanistan and
in Britain, Germany, India, the United States, and many
other countries. Journalists around the world scrambled to work their sources and reconstruct the sequence
of events, even as bloggers and pundits began to reflect
on their meaning and consequences. The world was
reminded—if it needed reminding—of the absurdities
that flow from armed conflict.

III

Both Dan and his friend Tom Little had long since
made known their wish to be buried in Afghanistan.
Dan and Tom's families resisted the U.S. embassy
proposal to return their bodies by military transport
to Dover Air Force Base. At the insistence of the FBI,
which was tasked with investigating the killings, their
bodies were taken to Baghdad for forensic autopsy and
then returned to Afghanistan.

The place in Kabul where foreigners are laid to rest
is itself a remarkable part of the story. Down a narrow lane in the Sherpur quarter of old Kabul, a stone's
throw from warlord mansions that bristle with weapons, is an imposing wall with an arched gate. Above a

patch of graffiti a sign reads, "British Cemetery." If one inquires in the shops opposite the graveyard, someone will call the caretaker, who will appear with an ancient key.

The cemetery's rough black door swings open upon an arresting scene. In the enclave, tended grass, rose-bushes, and peach trees intersperse the gravestones. The inscriptions and the plaques set into the perimeter wall not only mark the graves of the foreign dead but also serve as cairns that memorialize the saga of this land that so possessed Dan. Emissaries of empire, foot soldiers old and modern, seekers of fortune, explorers, scholars, pilgrims, ne'er-do-wells, entrepreneurs, unlucky travelers, and, more recently, humanitarians—these are all buried here. In Dan, many of these very impulses were distilled, except in this sense: if he was a warrior at all, it was a peace he waged.

That Dan was to be buried in what locals call the *Kabre Gora*, the "Foreigners' Cemetery," is poetic irony. As his neighbors in Hazara country and the Kabul bazaar had already declared, Dantri was most certainly Afghan.

Several weeks after the events in the Sharron Valley, family and friends assembled from distant corners of the world and gathered inside those walls to lay Dan Terry and Tom Little to rest amid the roses and the fruit trees. The service included messages of condolence from the government of President Hamid Karzai, the U.S. secretary of state, fraternal service organizations, and faith groups abroad.

But the most telling feature of the gathering was not the words of the great and the powerful. Rather, it was the silent throng of drivers and mechanics, welders and farmers, laborers and cleaners, shopkeepers, sweepers, and launderers who came in wordless, eloquent testimony to Dan's life. These were the ones whom Dan had touched. More importantly, these were the ones who had most deeply touched him.

IV

Although some groups of the Taliban and other jihadists opportunistically claimed responsibility for the killings, charging that the team had been "spying" or "proselytizing," the Taliban of Nuristan flatly rejected those assertions. The Nuristani Taliban, knowing that Dan and Tom and the others had come to serve the people of the Parun Valley, declared the killings a crime that they thoroughly disavowed. In response to that public riposte from the local Taliban, the overeager insurgent groups fell silent—an implicit admission that their charges were wildly off the mark and could never be substantiated to a disbelieving Afghan community.

Early speculation about a motive for the Sharron Valley killings centered on robbery. Both the local police and the FBI who opened an investigation first chalked up the killings to small-time banditry. While locals were aware of the growing presence of outside insurgents in that corridor of Badakhshan, the outside world knew little of this. Even Dan and Tom had not fully reckoned with this development when they weighed up the risks of their travel plan.

Although petty local thugs are the easiest to blame, the notion of robbery is quickly laid to rest by evidence from the scene of the crime. The camera-phone video footage taken as the Badakhshan police arrived to investigate the incident shows that most of the gear and personal possessions of the team remained in the vehicles, so systematic looting of what was easily portable cannot have been the main purpose of the killers. In fact, so limited was the skimming off of valuables, it was noted early on that Dan's hiking boots were among the few things missing.

Many of the team's personal possessions apparently went missing *after* the camera phone footage was shot, which suggests thievery after the Badakhshan police had arrived on the scene. By whom, it is not fully established, though some of the items were later recovered in local markets.

If highway robbery was not the primary motive of the gunmen, what else could their interest have been? The answers to this question, which must remain in the domain of speculation, rely upon small clues. We do know, for example, that when the gunmen were winding up their deadly work at the ambush site, their leader was shouting, "*Juldee, juldee!*" which means "Quickly, quickly!" in Urdu. Such reflexive usage would point not to local Afghans but across the border toward Pakistan. Furthermore, that the gunmen were reporting to a commander elsewhere by radio suggests the operation was carefully planned, with oversight from outside the immediate area.

Another factor points beyond what has been the practice of local groups, whether insurgents or thugs. A party of foreigners would represent a rich opportunity for ransom. While the outright killing of foreign aid workers in Afghanistan is not unknown, the usual practice has been to hold them in exchange for something of value, either payment in cash or the release of individuals held in detention as a quid pro quo. Summary killings of foreigners preclude any negotiated gain. What is more, the area's major players, both from the Kabul government and the Taliban, had granted their blessing to the team's plans and had established bonds of trust with Dan and Tom. That the Nuristani Taliban regretted the killings and condemned them openly also makes any local inspiration of the crimes unlikely.

If the plan and its execution came from outside the immediate area, who might have had an interest in mounting such an operation? Ideological reasons have sometimes been sufficient to justify the resources necessary for such a mission. Those who have researched the welter of jihadist groups in the region point to the Pakistani Taliban (or TTP), which is quite distinct from its Afghan counterpart; the Haqqani network; and perhaps like-minded groups such as the Hezb-i-Islami of Gulbuddin Hekmatyar, hero of the jihadist struggle against the Soviets. While Hekmatyar is Afghan, he has in recent times found himself adrift of the political process underway in Kabul, and he remains an outlier warlord with bases in Pakistan.

If ideology were the driving rationale for the killings, one would need look no further than some of those groups. Yet knowledgeable observers of the scene say that, as zealous as these groups may be, no such operation could be mounted without significant money changing hands. If that is true, then some hidden hand desiring to make an example of the team and possessing the resources necessary to make it happen orchestrated the events. Beyond that, everything is speculation.

While the fingerprints of an outside group, then, seem to be left on the killings, puzzling questions remain. Since the itinerary of the team had been quite flexible, it would have been difficult for anyone from a distance to know precisely what its route and timing might be. Furthermore, the killers had intimate knowledge of local geography, roads, and land features that permitted an efficient ambush. All of this would seem to indicate some degree of local participation.

Indeed, there are reports that Dan's prized hiking boots, taken from the scene of the killings, are being worn around in the mountains. Why, then, would the Nuristani Taliban not follow through on their promise to find and punish any locals who violated their assurances of safety to the medical team? The answer seems to be that any local participants in the crime, though they may be known to the Afghan Taliban, have powerful protectors elsewhere who would exact a fearsome cost should any harm befall their collaborators.

What this thicket of fact and supposition demonstrates is how tangled and lethal conditions of life in the Hindu Kush have become. The overlapping of vested interests, whorls of money, daily violence, opium, foreign players, illicit trade, and tribal politics are all realities that Afghans have to negotiate daily. That Dan survived in this miasma for thirty years is almost beyond belief.

It is still uncertain what became of Precious, Dan's one-of-a-kind mountain bike.

V

Dantri's Afghan friends tell story after story of how he pleaded for conciliation and dialogue when fiery passions and violence smoldered. He never tired of admonishing young people in Hazara country that "the pen is mightier than the rifle." During the winter famine, he took public satisfaction in the enacted parable: shovels cleared snowdrifts and picks and crowbars opened roads to bring life-saving food to starving communities. The firepower of guns could produce nothing to satisfy famished settlements.

During the era of warlord fighting, one account places him on a bridge between the defending Hazara militia and the besieging Taliban. A lone figure stands between the clamoring sides, beseeching the parties to cease their fire, lay down their weapons, and seek a peaceable arrangement that would avoid bloodshed.

In other stories, Dan vanishes into the backcountry for days at a time, interceding with tribal *shuras* for the release of captives and negotiating steps to ease rising tension and danger. (Those who know the details of these shadowy stories now languish in prisons or have fled abroad as fugitives and exiles.) Larger players in the national conflict would sometimes come to drink tea with Dan in the hope of gleaning insight and counsel on untying Afghanistan's Gordian knot.

Following the funeral at the British Cemetery in old Kabul and memorial gatherings in India, New York, and elsewhere, some felt that Dan's wild mountain life of peacemaking, service, altruism, and faith

deserved larger notice—a posthumous award, perhaps, or some kind of commemoration or honor. It
was mentioned that, while Dan had taken his place
humbly alongside less favored communities, he had,
after all, taken some pleasure when a major article on
Afghanistan in the February 2008 issue of *National
Geographic* ended by quoting his wisdom.

All of this the family pondered even as they grieved
the loss of their husband, father, and brother. What
course would keep faith with the highest of Dan's own
aspirations and ideals? One of Dan's daughters gave
voice to a dawning realization: if the news of any civic
honors or service awards should find its way back
to the Hindu Kush, and if that news should raise the
slightest doubt in the minds of Afghans about the moti-
vation behind Dan's years of friendship, it would do no
favor to the memory of his years of patient and joyful
peacemaking. No one should believe that Dan's drive
to live with and serve the people of Afghanistan came
at the behest of anyone but the Christ he followed.
Dan's motive in life, however inchoate or flawed its
outworking, was a selfless love schooled in faith and
attired in Afghan garb.

In the British Cemetery in Kabul, among the
stones commemorating history's storied adventurers,
warriors, entrepreneurs, and diplomats, a marker of
unpolished granite sets off a life in lavish service of
Afghan neighbors. The stone reads, "Above all, clothe
yourselves in love."

Afterword

Knotted into the Same Carpet

Sooner or later, the delegates of the contending forces, the diplomats, and the power brokers will gather. They will face each other across negotiating tables in search of an end to the frightful cost—moral, spiritual, and physical—of this present war in Afghanistan. After more than a decade of bloodletting in the Hindu Kush, the adversaries will have to make their way toward each other, past the war's wreckage, in search of common ground.

Who, then, will American and allied negotiators face when they take their places at those tables? A great deal of effort and resources are currently being expended to know the identities, styles, negotiating tactics, and goals of the Taliban emissaries. Scholars of Afghanistan who make it their business to follow such things are sketching out the probabilities, and their counsel is unsettling. In all likelihood, they tell us, the Western alliance diplomats will find themselves looking into the faces of some they once detained in secret prisons or at Bagram and Guantanamo; they will need to negotiate with those they have waterboarded or otherwise mistreated.

"In the end, we are all knotted into the same carpet," Dan Terry used to say—a muscular if elegant truth learned in broken mountain country. Whatever the human enterprise—whether probing the future of our communities, seeking to form strong families, or living peaceably as nations—we do well to remember that, when the moment of reckoning arrives, we will have to own up to our misdeeds as well as our strengths and, together with our adversaries, weave a carpet of shared life. If that is true, then the Taliban and Western societies, as well as their diplomats, will need to surmount the caricatures that have been imprinted on the public mind—those cartoon-like distortions of each other that have served the cause of war but that now thwart any path toward lasting peace.

If our delegates at those tables—and the rest of us, who sit at tables of our own where the future is being shaped—expect to move beyond the logic of naked power, beyond the smoke and grit of one-upmanship, we could do worse than this: to seek first, as did Dan Terry, a seat at the tea shop *samovar*, to find the places where ancient wisdom and prophecies are recited, places where friendships are formed and peace can be fashioned.

So let those who have called each other enemies draw up chairs at the *samovar*. There is an improbable friendship to be redeemed from the suffering and shadows.

Dan Terry, 1946–2010

The Author

Though born in Minnesota, Jonathan P. Larson's early home was the Brahmaputra River Valley of northeast India, amid the rice fields, bamboo groves, and tea gardens where Burma, Tibet, and India meet. The eldest of eight children, he studied at Woodstock School in the Himalayan foothills, where he was Daniel Terry's classmate and trekking partner. Following studies in history at the University of Minnesota, he and his childhood sweetheart, Mary Kay Burkhalter, married and moved to northeastern Congo (DRC) to teach school. In the DRC, the couple first encountered Africa's beauty, burdens, and promise and became parents of two daughters.

Following Jonathan's graduate studies, the family returned to Africa in 1981 under the auspices of the Mennonites to Botswana, on the doorstep of apartheid South Africa and the eve of what became the harrowing AIDS pandemic. Known for his grasp of Tswana language and lore, Jonathan served as a leadership trainer in African communities and churches. A third daughter was born in those years.

Based in Atlanta since 1994, Jonathan writes, mentors, and travels to conferences, campuses, and churches as storyteller and world citizen. Jonathan is a credentialed minister with the South East Mennonite Conference of Mennonite Church USA, and is a member of Berea Mennonite Church in Atlanta.